Our job in [...] who truly
inspires, who [...] things in
life. Rarely has anyone done that as well as Mickey Robinson. His is
a story of triumph out of tragedy, life out of death, and hope out of
despair. Mickey's story is a vital human document.

—Fred Griffith
Former ABC TV host, Cleveland Morning Exchange,
Cleveland, Ohio

Falling into Heaven is a true story that will impact every reader. What
so many people are longing for—love and peace—can be found in these
pages. Reading passages in this book recounting the early '70s transported me back to those special, God-ordained moments. I thank God
that I was there along with many others that our Lord had placed in
Mickey's path. This book is a testimony to what the power of God can
accomplish, even through the most difficult and challenging times.

—Phil Keaggy
Award-winning guitarist, singer, songwriter

Mickey Robinson inspires people to believe that with the supernatural God, all things are possible. I have known him and his family for
over thirty years. His message of hope has a dramatic effect on people
everywhere. In a time where multitudes are oppressed by fear and dis-
orientation, Mickey's story is a refreshing oasis of life. If you are seeking
guidance and power for your life, this book will help you get directed
on that path. We fear death because we do not have answers. Without
becoming theological, Mickey Robinson answers many of our questions
about the afterlife and, perhaps more importantly, he points us to our
eternal helper in this present life.

—Francis Frangipane
Author, teacher, and founder of In Christ's Image Training

Mickey Robinson's story is one of the most inspiring and engaging
stories you are likely to hear in your lifetime. It sizzles with supernatural
encounter. No matter where you may be on your spiritual journey, the

message in these pages will bring you face to face with a God of infinite love and compassion.

—Steve Fry
Senior Pastor, The Gate Fellowship, Franklin, TN

As a physician and surgeon, I am in awe of Mickey's story of supernatural healing and recovery. His recovery would be considered as much a miracle today as it was back in 1968. More importantly Mickey's story shows God's abundant grace and mercy, restoring hope and purpose, and launching Mickey and his wonderful wife, Barbara, into a ministry that has touched the nations. This life story of God's power to change tragedy into triumph will leave the reader marvelling at the God of wonders at work in our world today. Mickey's story can be anyone's story who puts their faith in Jesus Christ.

—Theodore Sawchuk, MD
Urologist, Fargo ND, Co-founder of Burning Hearts Ministry

Falling into Heaven is a powerful true-to-life message about a man who flew into the fires of destruction, only for them to be changed into the flames of transforming love. From a body caught in a raging fire, a heart was fashioned that will capture you. The contagious testimony and message of Mickey Robinson will grab your entire being and might be used to light a fire in you!

—James W. Goll
Founder of Encounters Network • Prayer Storm • G.E.T. eSchool

Our dear friend, Mickey Robinson, is one of the most passionate voices we know today. His near-death experience and heavenly encounter followed by a miraculous recovery brings hope and encouragement to anybody who hears it. We are thankful for what we've learned from Mickey's story and are convinced you will be too!

—Michael W. and Debbie Smith
Award-winning songwriter, recording artist, and author

Bonnie and I treasure the friendship that we have shared with Mickey and Barbara Robinson for over twenty-five years. We have seen few who walk with such authentic zeal for God and for all people. His miraculous recovery and accurate encouraging words of power have come to pass without fail for us and for many people. This book is a fruit of a life lived overcoming trials and tears with real joy. It is full of the testimony of the power of God's love and truth.

—Dr. Mahesh and Bonnie Chavda
International leaders and authors
Pastors of All Nations Church

Mickey's life has transcended the outer reaches of tragedy and triumph. His story will encourage and give hope to everyone who reads it. It is a must read for those who have reached the end of their own resources.

—Thomas S. Caldwell
Chairman, Caldwell Securities Ltd.

Mickey Robinson's life story is ineffable. I personally know Mickey and have been fortunate to work with him at many conferences. He is a man of character, talent, and prophetic wisdom beyond his years. He is a true voice for this generation! I am privileged to call him a friend.

—Paul Baloche
Award-winning songwriter, worship leader, and recording artist

Falling Into Heaven combines one of the most gripping, real-life, action-adventure narratives with a breathtaking account of the supernatural. Mickey's life is a literal beauty-from-ashes story of redemption, and needs to be heard by anyone with a pulse.

—Jordan Christy
Author of *How to Be a Hepburn in a Hilton World*

This is one of those books, that once you start reading, you don't want to put it down. It is an intense story about an intense man who is a passionate lover and follower of Jesus. I recommend the book and I recommend the man.

—Don Finto
Pastor Emeritus, Belmont Church, Nashville, TN
Founder, Caleb Company Ministries

You are about to meet a man who once fell from the heavens in flames, and who knows where you can touch the fire that heals from heaven. My friend is a walking miracle. Join him on his journey from a devastated life to one that greatly dares and dreams, and share with him the secret of his ongoing encounter with the resurrected Christ that has transformed multitudes.

—Winkie Pratney
International author and teacher

Falling

A Skydiver's Gripping Account

Into

of Heaven, Healings, and Miracles

Heaven

Mickey Robinson

BroadStreet
PUBLISHING

BroadStreet Publishing Group, LLC
Racine, Wisconsin, USA
www.broadstreetpublishing.com

Falling Into Heaven: A Skydiver's Gripping Account of Heaven, Healings, and Miracles

© 2014 Mickey Robinson

ISBN-13: 978-1-4245-4945-0 (print book)
ISBN-13: 978-1-4245-4949-8 (e-book)

Disclaimer from the author: This is my story and the book is true and as accurate as I can remember. In a few instances, I have changed the names to protect their privacy. While I believe God performs miracles today, my story includes the dedicated help of professional caregivers. This book is not intended as a substitute for the medical advice of physicians. It is unwise to ignore or not seek out the counsel of trained physicians. God works through the hands of doctors and the reader should regularly consult a physician in matters relating to his/her health and particularly with respect to any symptoms that may require diagnosis or medical attention.

Unless otherwise noted, all Scripture is taken from the New King James Version®. Copyright © 1982 by Thomas Nelson, Inc. Used by permission. All rights reserved. Scripture marked NASB is taken from the NEW AMERICAN STANDARD BIBLE®, Copyright © 1960,1962,1963,1968,1971,1972,1973,1975,1977,1995 by The Lockman Foundation. Used by permission. Scripture marked KJV is taken from the King James Version, which is in the Public Domain.

Cover design by Garborg Design Works, Inc. at www.garborgdesign.com
Typesetting by Katherine Lloyd, www.TheDESKonline.com

Stock or custom editions of BroadStreet Publishing titles may be purchased in bulk for educational, business, ministry, fundraising, or sales promotional use. For information, please e-mail info@broadstreetpublishing.com

Printed in the United States of America

Dedicated to my family

Michael

Matt and Natasha

Jacob and Sommer
Elijah, Shiloh, and Jorden

Bryan and Elizabeth
Ariel, Merci, and Ivy

You are my treasures

And to Barbara . . . a braver woman,
deeper vessel, truer beauty, vintage partner
I cannot imagine

Contents

Foreword by Don Piper

I t takes a great deal of courage to share an experience that challenges our notion of what is possible with God. I know a little something about that. In January of 1989, I was returning from a pastor's conference in East Texas when an 18-wheeler crossed the center stripe of a rural highway and hit my Ford Escort head-on. I was killed instantly, pronounced dead by four sets of paramedics, and found myself surrounded by God's glory in a place called heaven. Only a series of miracles and tens of thousands of fervent prayers allowed me to live and, eventually, regain most of my physical abilities.

I've had the pleasure of meeting Mickey Robinson numerous times. He and I have appeared on several television programs together to share our respective stories. Indeed, only a small cadre of people understand what it's like to stand in the presence of Almighty God outside the veil of this mortal body, and then return to relate their experiences. Mickey belongs to this band of brothers and sisters who allows faith and conviction to overcome doubt and skepticism. In this way, he is more than just my brother in Christ. He possesses a unique insight into what it's like to overcome unthinkable tragedy.

This book is a biography of a man who lived fast, fell hard, and rose humbled and healed by the mercy of a loving Savior. *Falling Into Heaven* will encourage you to believe in the power of prayer, the sufficiency of God's grace, and the strength of the human spirit. It is the story of a young man chasing worldly dreams, and a sovereign Creator who relentlessly seeks our affection. You will walk with Mickey during the highs and lows of growing up. You will understand his struggle to connect with a Heavenly Father that seems real but so far away. You will hurt with him as he endures unimaginable physical pain. You will rejoice in the miracles that stunned medical experts and confirm what the Bible tells us in Jeremiah 32:27, "I am the LORD, the God of all mankind. Is anything too hard for me?"

I am grateful to Mickey for allowing me to contribute a small part to a book that will undoubtedly strengthen the faith of thousands of believers and introduce many, for the very first time, to the saving power of faith in Jesus Christ. It is my sincere hope that Mickey's story will bless you as much as it has blessed me.

Don Piper
Author, *90 Minutes in Heaven*

Introduction

This book is a story about life—life seen through the eyes of a young man born the last half of the twentieth century. More change took place during this time in history than in all previous centuries combined. The population more than doubled. Technology, information, and knowledge increased and is now shared globally, as it happens! The post World War II society of America emerged—lavishly filled with freedom, prosperity, and unprecedented opportunities of power.

The ascent to achieve the American dream was dangled before this young man's eyes and mind, glamorously portrayed by movies, TV, movies, music, sports, and a handsome young American president. This brave new society also contained dark, ominous shadows of the Cold War, potential nuclear annihilation, and the breakdown of sound traditional values. The revolutionary aspect of the turbulent late '60s trumpeted free love, drugs, lawlessness, and "God-is-dead" or "God-is-whatever-you-want-your-god-to-be" belief systems.

The man this story is about grew up in the ideal, American, suburban, middle-to-upper-class dream. Even his street address, Pleasant Valley, gave the impression of near utopian, mid-American optimism.

However, his home life was plagued with family strife, alcoholism, and unpleasant disharmony. These conditions were not completely uncommon in that era; they were just more hidden and not talked about openly at that time.

Looking outside his family role models, he gravitated to a lifestyle of adventurous, live-for-the-moment pleasure seeking until his world was savagely interrupted by a tragic collision with human mortality.

At a point of utter hopelessness, he passed from this natural world into the spirit realm of the heavens. This heavenly encounter transcended the laws of time and physics, and he was transformed by the majesty of God's glory and power.

He returned to the earth with physical and emotional impossibilities to overcome that were met with healings, miracles, and supernatural spiritual guidance. This guidance and perilous journey occurred through the rough waters of a rapidly changing cultural shift. These conditions were overcome by the unchanging, unrelenting love of God. He was sent back to be a messenger—a messenger life and hope to all people. "I have slipped the surly bonds of Earth…and touched the face of God."[1]

I am that young man. This is my story.

One

Kiss the Sky

The walls of the factory glowed in the sweltering heat of summer. As humidity turned the Otis Elevator warehouse into a steam bath, workers moved like ants in a puddle of molasses.

Everyone, that is, except me.

I was nineteen years old, and not even eight hours of hard work could slow me down. I just put my body in gear until the four o'clock whistle blew, then launched out of that warehouse like a missile.

Turning the key on my '63 Ford, I heard a voice behind me.

"Hey, Mickey, you want to get a beer?"

"No. I have to get to the airfield," I said. "Another time maybe."

I didn't look to see who was talking before switching on the radio and grabbing a cigarette. As the squeal of an electric guitar pierced the air, I sped out of the parking lot and took any short-cut to get me home faster.

With Steppenwolf's *Born to Be Wild* playing loudly, the Ohio countryside became a green blur as the speedometer hit 90. The road stretched before me like a magic carpet. I caught my reflection in the rearview mirror. It was summer and I was tan, physically toned, highly focused, and motivated by a solitary purpose. One of my high school teachers, trying to get me to pursue an acting career, said the world was just waiting for me, but right then I didn't care about the world.

I was in love with the sky.

Just five months before, I'd jumped out of an airplane for the first time and floated to earth beneath an old, olive-drab military parachute. That jump was hardly spectacular, yet something amazing happened when I stepped into the sky that day. An unseen hand punched a delete button in my soul. From that moment on, everything in my life disappeared except the desire for more. More sky, more sensation, more speed.

Hurtling through ozone-drenched atmosphere at 125 mph filled me with more life and freedom than I'd ever known. *Free falling* was the right name for my new craving; I was passionately falling into freedom! In those elongated seconds before my parachute opened, there was no past and no future. No draft number. No Vietnam. No time clock. No boredom. No boundaries. If I could have injected free falling into my veins, I would have done it without a moment's hesitation.

As I pulled into the driveway, my thoughts were still consumed with this new love of my life. I took one last drag before flicking the cigarette over my shoulder. Standing on the front porch was my fourteen-year-old brother, leaning against the house, impatiently waiting for me with my packed parachute.

Leaving the radio playing full blast, I wordlessly bounded up the steps and brushed past him through the front door.

As soon as I entered the bedroom, I peeled off my work clothes and climbed into the clean, white jumpsuit that smelled of sky. As I grabbed my jump boots and started back down the hall, I caught a glimpse of my mother in the kitchen. She didn't turn around and I didn't stop. She knew I was in a hurry. I was always in a hurry.

My brother and I threw the parachute gear into the trunk

and took off for the country airport in a cloud of dust. As the speedometer climbed, I turned to him and said, "So…now you're grounded."

"Don't rub it in," he said with a pained look on his face. "It's a bummer they won't let me jump."

"Don't sweat it," I said. "You've got all the time in the world to fly. But yeah, it's a drag. We'll get it all worked out somehow."

My brother loved the sport as much as I did, but he was underage. Just a week before, an air traffic controller had gotten wise to his jumping and put his skydiving career on hold.

As we pulled into the Brunswick Flying Ranch, I spotted the Piper Cherokee 6 all gassed and ready to go. Although this wasn't much of an airport, it was convenient for me. A 2,200-foot runway and a plane were all I needed to support my habit. A small group of us were starting our own sky-diving operation and I was a partner in this new venture.

Walking from my car to the runway, I could feel all eyes on me. I enjoyed the special recognition. At my day job I was just a name on a time card, but here I belonged to a tribe of elite beings. The people watching were kind of skydiving groupies, and I was one of the rock stars of the group.

In every sport, people gravitate toward the ones who seem to stand out because they have "the right stuff." Well, I had the goods for skydiving. And I was feeling really cool about it.

"Hey, Superstar!"

I looked up into the grinning face of my friend and mentor, Dan. He was one of the first Americans to become a D-licensed skydiver after World War II. Dan was a living legend in a sport now being taken over by a new wave of extreme sport pioneers.

He'd recently initiated me into the mysteries of *relative work,* the highly synchronized maneuvers where skydivers join together at corresponding speeds. That evening Dan, Steve, and I were planning to jump at 13,500 feet and link together for a sixty-six-second free fall.

Also joining us for this flight would be two student jumpers. Our pilot, Walt, planned to let the first student out at 2,800 feet and then go on up to 4,000 feet so the other student could make a ten-second free fall.

All six of us were looking forward to trying out Walt's new aircraft. This Cherokee 6 promised to be excellent for skydiving, with plenty of power so we could get up to jump altitude quickly.

The farmland of Ohio spread around us like a golden quilt as we gathered in the shadow of the plane that hot August evening. As I breathed in the rich smell of summer hay, the falling sun set the earth ablaze with color.

Walt signaled that it was time to load up.

He'd removed all the seats except his pilot's seat from the plane, so there was room enough for all five skydivers and our equipment. As we climbed into the aircraft one at a time, I grabbed a place on the floor toward the back. I was just getting settled when I heard Steve call my name.

"Hey, Mickey, switch places with me, will you?

I moved forward to a spot on the floor beside Walt, who was now flipping switches and doing preflight checks. Finally he pulled back on the throttle and we started a quick sprint down the runway. Spotting my brother standing in the crowd, I gave him a grinning thumbs-up as the plane cruised by him like a convertible in a parade.

I thought I heard a strange noise. Was the engine sputtering slightly, or was it my imagination?

I listened again. The engine was purring loudly. I must have been mistaken. Settling back-to-back against another skydiver and resting my head against the fuselage, I closed my eyes. It would be a while before we reached 13,500 feet, so I decided to take a little catnap. I was never nervous before a jump. The closer I got to the actual moment, the more relaxed I became.

The drone of the engine and the extreme summer heat lulled me into a twilight sleep almost immediately. As I drifted off, I remembered something that had happened a few days before, when I'd gone to visit a friend at the hospital.

I was pretty unfamiliar with hospitals. They were dreary places full of sick people, and I couldn't wait to get out of there. Maybe it was the confinement that bothered me. But as I was leaving, I passed an old man slowly making his way down the hall. "Young man," he called out in a thick Middle Eastern accent.

I stopped and hesitantly turned around.

"You're a good-looking boy."

"Thank you," I stammered, a little embarrassed.

"You have such nice skin."

Without another word, he turned and continued tottering down the hall. I smiled and stole a glance at my tanned forearm. I always glowed like a beach bum in the summer.

I was jolted awake when Walt pulled the throttle wide open for takeoff. My body leaned like a sack of cement into the back of the skydiver beside me.

I shook my head a few times to clear away the memory of that old man. Taking a deep breath as I looked around, I was relieved to find myself in the cockpit of an airplane rather than the hallway of that hospital. *Having to spend even one day in a place like that would give me the creeps.*

The aircraft picked up speed, and soon I felt the wheels pull away from the asphalt. Still a bit drowsy, I sensed the pilot had pulled way back on the stick, resulting in an unusually steep climb. Walt was impressed with the performance of his week-old aircraft, and he was particularly enjoying the speed and power of this takeoff.

But then, still at low altitude, there was a strange sound.

Silence.

The engine died and we lost all of our lift, plunging to the ground at a horrific speed. We were experiencing an aerodynamic stall. Walt frantically tried to restore power, but it was no use. There were no options. The engine was gone.

"That's it!" he cried. "We're going down!"

Because we'd been ascending at such a steep angle, there was no gliding forward, no chance of even making a crash landing. As the nose of the aircraft pitched forward, we dropped to earth like a broken toy.

A huge tree loomed in front of the cockpit window. There was no time to brace myself. I didn't even have time to swallow before the Cherokee 6 took full impact on its wing and midsection against a tree, hurtling me forward and slamming my face against the instrument panel. As the plane cartwheeled before skidding to a stop on its belly, the ruptured fuel tank spewed gasoline throughout the cockpit.

I lay there barely conscious for a few moments before the splattered fuel ignited into flames. As if in a dream, I felt pieces of the burning, melted material falling on me. I waved my arms back and forth in a weak attempt to brush away the hot, sticky debris.

I didn't know which end was up. My mind was numb except for the stabbing impulse to escape. A voice in my head kept screaming, *Get out!* but my body couldn't respond.

When I saw light pouring through the torn fuselage, I frantically pushed one leg through the hole to try to exit the plane. But my parachute equipment was caught on something behind me. No matter how hard I twisted or heaved, I was going nowhere.

Stuck like a fly in a web of burning metal, the adrenaline finally reached my gut and coaxed a sound from the only part of me that wasn't numb. If it hadn't been for my screams, I would have burned to death.

Until then, no one had realized the pilot and I were trapped in the cockpit. With only minor injuries, the other four skydivers had exited the plane immediately after it skidded to a stop. But on his way out, Dan stopped for a split-second to glance toward the cockpit. He saw Walt move but heard no cries for help, so he assumed we were both okay and would be following him out of the plane.

Dan was just a few yards from the wreckage when he heard a loud *whoosh* followed by the terrified screaming of a man on fire. Going back into that plane was like running toward a bomb ticking off its last seconds. Still, he ran toward the sound of my voice.

The pilot's seat had crunched forward on impact, jamming it under the instrument panel. Walt moaned in pain while I screamed for help, each of us oblivious to the other's deadly predicament.

I didn't see Dan enter the cockpit. My jumpsuit and equipment were soaked with fuel and on fire when I heard his familiar voice say, "Help me, Mickey. Help me!" I twisted with my last ounce of strength as two inhumanly strong arms heaved me out of the wreckage. With his bare hands, Dan slapped at the flames burning my head and neck while screaming over his shoulder, "I'll be back for you, Walt! Undo your seatbelt!"

Dan let go of me to run back inside. In that second, the left wing, which had been drained empty to reduce weight, exploded.

I somehow managed to stagger fifteen feet farther away before my fuel-drenched jumpsuit ignited again. I collapsed on the ground. Immediately Dan was at my side, rolling me back and forth until the last flame was quenched.

I lay next to the burning plane, smoldering like a coal fallen from a furnace. "How bad?" I whispered. "How bad am I?" The words rasped out of my throat as the right side of my face was horribly burned.

"Can't tell, Mickey," Dan responded. "Don't talk. Just lie still."

I heard sirens and running footsteps and roaring like the sound of a bonfire after a homecoming game. The air was thick with the stench of gasoline and burning debris. Snakes of black smoke crawled in the sky above me, and faces floated in and out of view like human clouds.

Something was soothing the fear and numbing the pain. I was sinking into the peace of perfect shock, a merciful hand lifting me out of my tormented body.

As white fingers slid an oxygen mask over my face, my blackened flesh peeled off and slid onto the ground. Someone carried me through flashing red lights and thudding doors until I couldn't see the sky anymore.

As the whine of an ambulance pierced the air, pictures beat against my brain like birds escaping from a cage. My father's face as he caught the biggest fish of his life…my mother's small hands clutching rosary beads…Mickey Mantle slamming a ball out of the stadium and into the stars.

Then I saw a boy standing on a windy hill. It was me. But my intimate romance with the sky in free fall was brutally terminated when we hit the ground.

This must be the end.

I had no way of knowing it was just the beginning.

Two

Man in a Shadow

Standing fearlessly at the top of Midland Boulevard, roller skates strapped to my feet and tattered window shade in hand, I was ready for takeoff. I was only seven years old, but in a few seconds I'd be soaring high above the neighborhood. Looking down the hill, I was gathering the courage to launch out in this gale-force wind on my first flying adventure.

Ten...nine...eight...seven...

As I counted the seconds until takeoff, I half-hoped someone would step up to salute me on my first flight ever. But I was alone as I unfurled the shade and abandoned myself to the wind.

The clatter of skates on cement numbed my ears and made my teeth chatter as I rolled faster and faster down the hill. The billowing shade whipped and twisted wildly in the wind until, all of a sudden, I couldn't hear my skates anymore. Was I...? Maybe...Yes! I was airborne! Come on, come on, higher, higher!

A flash of white light. Had I reached the clouds already?

The next thing I remember was being sprawled out on the concrete. Blinking, I reached behind my head and felt a knot the size of a golf ball on my aching skull.

Without a word I unstrapped my skates, swallowed hard, and trudged up the hill like Orville Wright on a windless day. Just before reaching home, I plunged the wounded shade into a garbage can.

But I never trashed my dream of flying. I still believed Albert Einstein would come up with an anti-gravity formula, something like the little white pill that made smoke when I dropped it into my electric train.

After all, this was 1956.

As television fed me on its soft white bread of wonder, I anxiously awaited the coming of our brave new world. It was right around the corner, and I was definitely going to be part of it. Today the sidewalk, tomorrow the moon!

Already planning my next flight, I jerked open our kitchen door and grabbed a bottle of Coke. As I planted myself in front of the television, the swamp-green screen glimmered into a black-and-white image.

Suddenly there he was—the man of steel.

Able to leap tall buildings in a single bound, faster than a speeding bullet, more powerful than a locomotive, Superman was the hero of every seven-year-old kid in America. As I watched him fly through the air, I couldn't sit still. After grabbing a towel and tying it around my neck, I leapt onto the armrest of our living room sofa and dove off of it repeatedly.

"Mickey!"

Uh-oh. A lethal dose of kryptonite in the form of my mom!

"Get down from there! How many times have I told you not to stand on the furniture? And not to use my clean towels. Do you understand? Next time you use my clean towels, no more Superman!"

As she walked into the kitchen, Mom added, "Your father has to go back to the shop this afternoon. He wants you to go with him."

It was a fate worse than death to be stuck with my dad on a summer afternoon. Most fathers would take their kids to baseball games, or at least to the bowling alley. Not mine. He made me sit there while he drank whiskey and played cards in some dingy bar.

I don't know why he always took me with him on those little outings. Maybe it was the only way he knew how to be a father.

As I took my usual place on a vinyl barstool with a bag of potato chips and a shot glass full of cherries, I studied the man who lived in my house and called himself Mike Robinson.

My dad.

He was the youngest of six sons born to Michael and Eva Rochovitz. Born in St. Petersburg, Florida, in 1912, my father had changed his name from Rochovitz to Robinson in order to slide more tastefully into the ethnic stew that is called America.

He got his wish and moved right into the middle class. A machinist with four kids and a mortgage, Mike Robinson was the carefree guy next door who always worked too late and drank too much. I knew my dad was an intelligent man, even though he bragged about stuff he knew like history and world politics. He often resorted to wisecracks and political potshots.

The real Mike Robinson was hidden away where no one could touch him, and not until I was a grown man did I uncover one of his personal secrets. At age eighteen, during the Depression, my father made a terrible mistake that resulted in being sentenced to eleven years in prison for stealing $2.50 from a cash register. This was a crushing blow in his life. No matter how much he drank or how hard he worked, he was never able to overcome the shame of those Depression years.

Like so many Americans in the '50s, haunted by memories of war and loss, my father was a man on the run. Running from failure, he became a workaholic. Running from his heritage, Michael Rochovitz became Mike Robinson. Running from his past, he became an alcoholic. Running from himself, he became a man in a shadow.

And an embarrassment to me.

I wanted to be proud of my dad, but I hated his crude humor

and rough manners. Watching him in that dark bar, smelling of cigarettes and bourbon, I wanted to be nothing like him.

Mike Robinson had the opposite of the Midas touch. Everything he touched turned to brass. Try as he might, he couldn't connect the dots on the picture of family life.

Although he and my mother shared a home, they might as well have existed on separate planets. She refused to live anywhere but Cleveland, but he never stopped talking about moving to Florida. She was a realist who went to mass. He was a dreamer who went fishing.

As the years went by, my mother's frustration had a volatile effect on my smoldering father. I was afraid to bring friends home because I never knew when sparks would fly.

I watched my father walk an increasingly thin line between silence and rage. This became very clear to me the Christmas he gave me my dream come true, a Daisy BB gun. I couldn't believe my luck as I greedily unwrapped the slender package. My eyes must have been the size of baseballs as I held the coveted gift in my hand.

"Thanks, Dad!"

Reaching over to help me, he made sure I attached only the barrel that shot corks and not the one that shot BBs.

"When you're old enough to be responsible, I'll let you shoot BBs," said Dad in that I-know-what's-best-for-you tone of voice.

Yet, as the excitement of Christmas Day took its toll on a trigger-happy little kid, the inevitable happened. I shot a cork and accidentally hit my brother, who howled like he'd been hit by a cannonball.

I knew my dad would be mad, but I didn't expect what happened next. I could actually feel the heat of his anger as he grabbed the gun out of my hand and bent it into a horseshoe over the back of the couch. I didn't say a word as I helplessly watched the best Christmas present I had ever gotten turned into a piece of junk.

Later he felt bad about losing his temper, but it was too late. Something inside me broke right along with that gun. When my friends asked me what I got for Christmas, I pretended nothing had happened.

Pretty soon I became an expert at pretending. I turned a deaf ear to my parents' quarrels. I ignored the broken windows and broken promises. I closed the door on all the skeletons in the Robinson family closet and spent my time elsewhere.

Our house at 6708 Pleasant Valley Road became little more than a pit stop where I ate, slept, and changed clothes. There was too much pain throbbing within those walls, so I unplugged myself from the family unit and turned toward the carefree world of friends and adventure.

I never tired of exploring the maple jungles of Ohio with my neighborhood pals. Together we found the tallest tree in the woods and built a tri-level fortress worthy of Robin Hood. In the topmost branches, we built a giant slingshot out of an old bicycle inner tube to protect ourselves from little sisters, inquisitive mothers, and enemy tribes. When the alarm sounded, we'd head for the top of the tree to rain crab apples down on the intruders.

Life was simple. There was no obstacle I couldn't outclimb, outrun, or outwit. The observation deck of our tree house was the highest place I'd ever been, and sitting up there gave me an intoxicating sense of freedom. The world looked completely different from fifty feet up, and I never wanted to come back down.

Mine was the generation of high hopes, while my parents had come from the generation of hard times. Although my mother and father were able to survive the harsh reality of the Depression, something of life had been wrung out of them.

As a child of the '50s, I couldn't understand the hope-killing hardship they had endured. I just assumed they didn't know how to have fun.

Although there weren't many "Kodak moments" for the Robinson family, there was one sacred pleasure my father and I were always able to share. Every summer he drove us to a lake in Canada so we could do something together as a family. Fishing was his religion of choice and it was one part of my father's world I was invited to enter.

Each morning we walked silently from our cabin through the cool, gray mist to the waiting water. There we performed the ancient ritual of loading poles and nets and boxes into an old bait-stained motorboat. As my father coaxed a sputter from the outboard, I pushed off from the dock into a world where we were no longer father and son.

On the lake, Dad wasn't old and I wasn't young. He wasn't distant and I wasn't ashamed. In that timeless place, we were just two fishermen waiting for silver creatures to float up through the dark water like manna from the deep.

We didn't talk much. We didn't need to talk. It was enough being silent together. We sat on opposite ends of the boat from dawn until dusk, Dad feverishly absorbed in his quest for a mighty muskie while I waited for a walleye or bass to strike my hook.

I think the closest my father ever came to knowing peace was in that boat. It will always be my happiest memory of him. I don't know if he thought about God in those days. It wasn't something we talked about. I don't know if he even thought about eternity, but if he did, I'm sure his vision of heaven was a cold mountain lake brimming with fish.

On that lake, everything he touched turned to gold. He held the lodge record for muskie and even had an article written about him in the *Cleveland Plain Dealer*. I was proud of my dad's success as a fisherman, even though he couldn't make it as a family man. Maybe that was because he was a dreamer married to a realist…a realist whose vision of heaven had nothing to do with fish.

Three

The Bells
of St. Michael's

My mother's vision of heaven was an altar where her four children stood before God in crisply ironed clothes and perfectly polished shoes. As a good Catholic, she believed her job was to raise God-fearing children who would someday produce plenty of God-fearing grandchildren. And so my brother, two sisters, and I each dutifully entered Catholic school at the tender age of six.

It was at St. Michael's in Independence, Ohio, that I met the God who walked softly and carried a big stick, but it was also there I met the God who inspired awe and wonder in my little-kid heart. Each Sunday morning as I followed my mother up those ominous stone steps, I felt like an ant crawling into Yankee Stadium. Everything was huge and shiny and holy. I would shudder a little going near the huge statue of Michael the archangel that stood next to the Gothic front entrance of our church building. I was afraid if I so much as brushed his foot, the lifeless head might turn and stare into my murky little soul.

With Brylcreem-combed hair and a white shirt buttoned almost to my eyeballs, I dipped my fingers in holy water while glancing painfully at my sister Marilyn. Standing there, politely clutching a pink rosary in her white-gloved hand, she looked like a miniature adult. And that's what we were expected to be until mass was over. Until we descended those stone steps, there would be no whispering, no pinching, and no giggling—only pious silence.

It's a little tough being pious when you're seven, but I didn't feel much like a kid as I gazed at the suffering Jesus on the Stations of the Cross. Those pictures made me feel like I was staring out the car window at the scene of an accident. Yet the passionate suffering of Jesus Christ was being permanently written inside me.

Mass was the only time I ever saw my mother sitting down as she rigidly followed the order and ritual of mass. I thought she was the only woman on earth who could straighten my collar, pick lint off my sister's dress, and make the sign of the cross at the same time. My mother was fiercely determined to present her children without spot or wrinkle.

My mother wasn't overly soft, yet she held our family together with blood, sweat, and tears. With little or no control over my father's downward spiral, she poured every bit of her amazing energy into keeping floors waxed and kids polished.

Secretly gazing at her in the half-light of the sanctuary, I could see the strain in her face. Though barely forty, my mother's countenance showed the weight of a difficult marriage. Yet Jean Gillombardo Robinson was the faithful daughter of Sicilian Catholics, and nothing could stop her from attending church. Although my father rarely joined us, except on Christmas and Easter, my mother never missed a Sunday mass.

As our little family sat quietly in the ruby and emerald light pouring down from the stained-glass windows, I felt a holy hush.

I had no trouble believing I was in God's house; I just had trouble picturing this person called God. I couldn't talk to Him except through a priest, and I couldn't tell him about baseball or Superman. The priest only wanted to talk about sin.

I couldn't understand God because He only spoke Latin. I

couldn't tell Him about my dream of flying because He wanted kids to sit still and keep quiet.

I couldn't touch Him, but at an early age I was taught He wanted me to eat His body and drink His blood. That was weird, but still I was intrigued in a seven-year-old kind of way.

I spent my first year in catechism getting ready to meet God. It was kind of like Catholic boot camp, where the nuns led us through rigorous training for First Confession and First Communion. It sounded simple enough. First we confessed our sins and then God came down to fill us with "sanctifying grace." The nuns taught us in first grade that if we died in a state of sanctifying grace we'd go straight to heaven.

I didn't know what that was, but I was more than ready to be filled with it. I thought communion would be like the time Jimmy and I pricked our fingers and let the blood run together, except this time the sanctifying grace would run together with the wine to make me and God blood brothers.

When the big day finally arrived, my collar was buttoned so tightly my white communion outfit looked like a little tuxedo. While marching single file down the church aisle with the other kids, I was seized with terror.

All of a sudden I knew I couldn't do this right. It wouldn't take more than one little fight with my sister to blow my First Communion. I just knew I was going to sin again and lose my sanctifying grace.

I was headed straight for the back of the church building. What to do?

I came upon a perfect plan. While walking back to my seat, I would make a beeline out of the church and head straight for Highway 21. There an oncoming car would squash me flat and beam me to heaven before I had a chance to lose my sanctifying grace.

I breathed a sigh of relief. It was the only way to make it into eternity without having to sit around wasting time in purgatory. I had a sneaking suspicion purgatory would be like the dentist's office—a weird white waiting room where you sweated bullets while listening to some kid scream for mercy down the hall. I had to make a run for it. Sanctifying grace or bust!

But when the time came for my heroic sacrifice, I chickened out. Walking dutifully back to the pew, I became just another church kid who knew what to do and when to do it. Yet I still didn't know God—not like I knew about Mickey Mantle, a god of flesh and blood whose batting average was engraved forever in my heart.

I could soar in sports, but my Catholic career was a different story. I was continually tormented by my imagination. Whenever I lied, had an impure thought, or did anything wrong that fell into the category of sin, I was clueless to find the way out.

Each time I received the communion wafer dipped in wine, I sat in the pew afterward with my fingers pressing hard against my eyeballs until colored lightning streaked the darkness. Staring into this colored kaleidoscope there were always blue dots mixed in with the colors, and these I associated with sin. The more blue dots, the more sin in my life.

There were way too many blue dots, probably because my mind refused to shut up. It kept tapping me on the shoulder every Sunday morning and whispering, *I'm hungry.*

Everyone was required to fast before communion, and as soon as mass ended I zoomed out of the church at breakneck speed and headed straight for Breck's Drug Store. There I jammed pretzel logs in my mouth while gulping a chocolate Coke.

No matter how many prayers I prayed or confessions I made, I couldn't skate around God the way I skated around everything else. My quick wit and confidence earned me the status of *cool* among the neighborhood kids, but these qualities didn't seem to impress God.

So I learned to fake it, and no one seemed to know the difference. Not until that day in the fourth grade when I had a close encounter with Father John.

Father John was a Polish priest who made Superman look like a wimp. This man was 6'3" and 240 pounds with a voice right out of the Old Testament. Not the kind of priest a kid wants to meet in a dark confessional.

When the little window slid open, my heart would melt like a popsicle. But in the next instant, I'd straighten up to meet the challenge. I could always fake my way through confession by reciting a laundry list of sins that I made up while waiting in line—though nothing more grisly than being mean to my little brother or talking back to my parents.

"Bless me, Father, for I have sinned."

"When was your last confession?"

"Last Wednesday, I think."

"What confession do you have to make, my son?"

"Um, I...I was disobedient to my mom."

So far, so good. I sprinted through the basic stuff and then jumped right into the prayer called the act of contrition. I was in the homestretch. I had recited this prayer so many times I could do it while standing on my head shuffling baseball cards.

"I..."

Uh-oh. Mental Jell-O. I went completely blank. How could I fake the prayer of contrition in front of a 240-pound priest? Seconds ticked by like hours. I slid both hands over my mouth, closed my eyes, and swayed back and forth while mumbling the lyrics to my favorite song.

Slowly this huge, shadowy figure on the other side of the confessional sat up in his chair and stopped me in mid-mumble. "Young man!" he bellowed.

Oh, God, kill me now! "Yes, Father?"

"Do you know what you're praying?"

"Uh…"

"Do you realize you're talking to *God*?"

As he said the word *God*, I was certain that Charlton Heston was standing right outside the confessional, waiting to bludgeon me with a stone tablet.

"Without the prayer of contrition, there is no forgiveness for your sin. Do you understand that, young man?"

Oh boy, did I!

"And don't you ever forget that, as long as you live!"

"No, Father. I won't." I choked the words out past the jagged lump in my throat.

Somehow I made it through confession, but once outside I exploded in tears of embarrassment. From that day on, I did everything in my power to avoid Father John. Still, he'd made an indelible impression on me. I never again forgot the prayer of contrition.

A few months later, Sister Teresa talked to me about becoming an altar boy. The teachers let me out of class during school to practice with the experienced altar boys. Rookies had very little responsibility during the mass. I was, however, given my own cassock: a black robe buttoned clear down to my ankles. I brought it home and showed my mom.

The next day I got the bad news that my first mass was to be officiated by Father John the Terrible!

Somehow I made it through the week and showed up at mass with my fingers clenched around the bell. My job was to ring it at appropriate moments when there was a long pause in the priest's prayer. It was only supposed to be a couple of times—a simple task for anyone who didn't have an ocean of adrenalin pouring through him.

I stood there calmly as Father John went to the altar of the sanctuary with us behind him. I waited there quietly as he spoke in Latin. When he breathed, I rang that bell like I was Mickey Mantle hitting a homer! Father John glanced at me with a strained expression. I assumed he wanted me to ring harder. So I did.

Every time he so much as blinked an eye, I rang that bell. It must have sounded like Santa Claus caught in the spin cycle of a Maytag washer, but I didn't care. With a terrified look on my face, I kept ringing for dear life. By the end of that mass, Father John looked a little scared himself.

And so I stumbled through my Catholic boyhood with a little grace and a lot of determination. Already skilled in the art of survival, I was the kid who could come out of any playground scrape with my hair combed and collar buttoned. Not until I was more than eleven years old did I encounter anything I couldn't overcome with brains, luck, or charm.

That year a friend sneaked one of his father's *Playboy* magazines out of the house and brought it to school. He was risking certain death by doing this, but the nuns never caught him. When school was over, a small group of us headed straight for the far corner of a vacant lot.

Gathering into a tight, guilty little circle, we passed the magazine from sweaty palm to sweaty palm. When it came my turn, I opened the magazine. As my eyes took their first glance at a naked woman, a clammy feeling clutched my neck.

The pictures made me excited and afraid, like sitting in a scary movie with one eye open and the other eye closed. I wanted to look, but I also wanted to turn away.

Something strange settled in my soul that day. I felt a forceful, powerful excitement and also a fear of being caught. I knew it was wrong but it felt so good. There was no hope for absolution since I'd far rather lie like a rug than tell a priest about that magazine.

There was no way out. I had to live with what I had done.

Months went by and I never mentioned this sin to anyone—until the day a young priest visited St. Michael's on his way to a mission post in South America.

He came out on the playground at recess to talk to us, and there was something different about him. He wasn't a voice behind a shadowy screen, but a real human being sitting next to me on the steps. He didn't stare down at me, but looked directly into my eyes. He didn't call me *son*. He called me Mickey.

Pretty soon my friends and I began telling him things we'd never told another adult. Strangely, he didn't say anything. He just listened. Before I knew it, the cat was out of the bag.

"Father, I looked at a *Playboy* magazine."

I don't know what I expected next—chords crashing on a piano or trains going through a tunnel. Thunder at the very least. Instead I felt an incredibly gentle hand cover my head as the young priest made the sign of the cross, closed his eyes, and spoke a prayer in Latin. I have no idea what he said, but in that moment something changed in me. I felt the shame melt away, as though the sun had come out on a winter day.

All my friends who talked to him said things like "Didn't he make you feel good?" None of us had ever met anyone who could make us comfortable opening up about such an awkward thing.

I never forgot what happened that day. It was the first time I felt freedom shine through the stiffness of rules and regulations.

Although it seemed like God still lived way out in space, I felt like He'd just paid a little visit to my playground.

Four

The Need for Speed

O n a cold January day in 1961, I watched spellbound as our
handsome new president took the oath of office. JFK had
a perfect smile and lots of hair, which already put him way out in
front of Eisenhower. But when I heard him say early in his presi-
dency that America would put a man on the moon before the end
of the decade, he became my hero.

John Fitzgerald Kennedy was everything I wanted to be—an
important guy who played football, looked like a movie star, and
talked about outer space. I studied in detail the development of
our space program. I knew all about the seven Mercury astronauts and the hardware of the NASA space program. I followed
it all in detail—Alan Shepard's fifteen-minute suborbital flight,
Gus Grissom's flight in which the capsule sank. I explained the
details of the Mercury program and led discussions in school as
we watched on TV the Ohio native John Glenn first orbit the
earth. I basked in the power and glory of the space program. I
inhaled facts the way other kids ate peanuts. My bedroom was
plastered with magazine photos of astronauts, moon modules,
and rocket launches. My dad subscribed to *National Geographic*
magazine and I practically memorized everything about the space
program.

If I'd been a kid in 1861, I would have packed my bags and
headed west for adventure. But the West didn't sound so wild to

me anymore. Space wasn't just the *final* frontier; it was the *only* frontier for a kid like me.

This was an awesome decade for becoming a teenager. The air hummed with possibilities, even if I never became an astronaut. But no one imagined one of the most memorable sounds of the '60s.

One evening in 1962, while watching TV with my brother, the gray face of Walter Cronkite flashed onto the screen. "We interrupt this program to bring you a special report."

I turned the TV up and called my dad. Special reports were few and far between, so when they appeared, America listened.

"Today President Kennedy demanded that Nikita Khrushchev, premier of the Soviet Union, remove all nuclear missiles from Cuba. Until this demand is met, the president has ordered a full naval blockade of that island."

All I needed to hear was the word *nuclear* to set my imagination soaring. Being a naturally inquisitive kid with a bent toward science, I had poured over civil defense bulletins and studied everything I could about nuclear war. I even stored cans of food in our basement so we could live on chicken noodle soup while civilization melted away.

Unlike most kids my age, I knew what the word *firestorm* meant. So the next day on the playground, I held a summit meeting with my three best friends. Together we called ourselves The Four Aces. Maybe it was because the four of us were a popular band of brothers; I think we were inspired by the movie *West Side Story*.

We had each chosen an ace from a deck of cards and then brazenly pasted it into the back of our school notebooks. I was the Ace of Diamonds and for some reason this title made me feel responsible for the welfare of the kids in our school. I had to be a leader in times of crisis, and this was definitely one of those times. I knew if the Russians pushed a button, more than 100 million people would be dead in half an hour.

"What should we do, Mickey?" asked my friend Chuck, aka the Ace of Hearts. "You think we oughta put our stuff in the basement?"

I looked at him in disbelief. Obviously this kid had no idea what a fifty-megaton blast followed by a 250 mph fire-wind would do to our nice little neighborhood. I was about to answer him with a snide remark when, all of a sudden, I had an idea. "Hey, wouldn't it be cool if we made one last confession before it's too late?"

My friends looked like I'd just suggested we eat liver and Brussels sprouts for lunch.

"Why would you wanna do that, Mickey?"

"I don't want to die with unconfessed sins. Do you?"

"I guess not."

So with the zeal of Jesuits on their way to martyrdom, The Four Aces marched across the playground toward the rectory. Normally, I wouldn't be caught dead going there of my own free will. The rectory was a weird, off-limits kind of place—the habitation of really serious black-robed priests. But today I felt it was necessary. There's something about nuclear war that makes a guy feel like getting right with God.

When I knocked on the big wooden door, it opened slowly, like the door in *The Addams Family* show. The monsignor calmly listened to our urgent request, then without a word led us back toward the eerie confessional.

This time I wasn't kidding around. The nuns' teaching left no doubt in my mind that I could face either a priest or eternal judgment. If Khrushchev pushed that button, I was only moments away from having to tell God my deepest, darkest secrets. So when it came my turn, I gladly spilled my guts to the priest.

When we stepped back outside, the world felt safer. It even smelled better. Although America was still on red alert, fear and worry had been lifted from me. Years later, I read that Kennedy had looked out from the White House balcony that same day and thought, *Tomorrow this will all be gone.* That's how close we were to a nuclear exchange.

But I was thirteen years old, and as soon as this crisis passed, I turned my attention back to the business of growing up.

Only six months later, my Catholic school career came to an end. Standing by the mirror in my uniform that June day in 1963, I felt like a soldier being honorably discharged from duty. I couldn't wait to exchange the weird green tie and gray pants for civilian clothes. I'd served my time at St. Michael's and was now being promoted to the rank of teenager.

That summer I got my first paycheck from my job at Dairy Queen, making sundaes for ninety cents an hour. I ate all the mistakes and put all my paychecks right in the bank.

I entered Independence High School as a ninth grader. No Catholic school uniforms were required, so I started buying my own clothes with my own money. Having the right look was important for my image.

One of the items I purchased that fall was a hooded fur parka that made me look like an Italian Eskimo. Definitely one of a kind, it was made from some weird polyester that resembled the pelt of a mouse on chemotherapy. I was proud of that coat, but my father saw it as another excuse to needle me about my appearance. He never missed an opportunity to make fun of my desire to look good.

"Hey, pretty boy, you better look in the mirror. I think you've got a hair out of place."

Outwardly I ignored him, but inwardly I counted the days. I couldn't wait to really be on my own.

I still went to mass, but it became just a duty I performed. Church had long ago lost its childhood aura of awe and wonder. As far as I was concerned, going to mass was merely a family obligation—something everybody else did as well.

But my nice little formula took a direct hit on November 22, 1963. My study hall teacher asked me to take some papers to the principal's office, but when I got there the secretary looked like she'd just seen a ghost.

"President Kennedy has been shot!" she cried.

I thought she was kidding. Things like this didn't happen in my version of America. I ran back to study hall and told my teacher, who promptly announced the news to a bunch of bewildered ninth graders. Amid all the guys with varying theories and all the girls in tears, I kept saying over and over, "How could this happen?"

JFK did everything right. How did Smart + Handsome + Rich + American + Catholic + President = Getting shot in the head at forty-six? This did not compute. And where was God?

The weirdness got weirder. On Sunday morning before church, I watched with millions of others as the accused assassin, Lee Harvey Oswald, was gunned down in the Dallas police station on national television. Skeptical and confused, I sat in church, wondering why we even bothered to pray. If God couldn't protect Kennedy, maybe He couldn't protect anybody.

An empty feeling crept over me every time some girl said, "Isn't Jackie brave?" Television commentators repeated the words *Dallas* and *Oswald* for what seemed like forever. Was this the beginning of reality TV?

The shadow of national mourning drove me crazy. America had just lost not only the president but also her innocence. The blood in Dallas stained our hearts and our half-masted flag.

I had to get busy with something to block out my fourteen-year-old confusion, so during Christmas vacation I caught a ride to a ski area that had just opened not far from Independence.

Although I'd always been a kamikaze sledder tearing down our neighborhood hills, growing up in Ohio had robbed me of my rightful place in the American legend. Surely if I'd grown up in Colorado, Jean-Claude Killy would have trembled at the name Mickey Robinson.

Walking into the ski shop in my rabbit-fur parka and corduroy pants, I looked like Nanook of Cleveland. I plunked down my hard-earned money to rent skis, boots, and poles, then headed for the rope tow.

I was just about to climb on when I heard a familiar voice call my name. I turned and saw Val, an old classmate from St. Michael's. She came from a pretty well-to-do family and was obviously no stranger to the sport. She definitely outclassed me in her stretch pants and baby blue parka, but I was too excited to care about anything except getting to the top of that hill.

"Hey, Val! How ya doin'?"

"Is this your first time skiing?"

The numbers painted on my boots must have given me away. "Yeah, I'm headed for the beginner's slope. You?"

She smiled. "Not really. Why don't you come with me? I'll teach you everything you need to know."

It didn't take much to convince me. We rode the T-bar up to the intermediate run and Val coaxed me down the first part of the slope. She skied slowly back and forth ahead of me while calling out instructions on how to traverse and form a snowplow.

"You're doing great, Mickey! You can make it by yourself from here on. I'll meet you at the bottom."

As Val disappeared, I focused on following her instructions, thinking, *This is easy.* I was just starting to get comfortable on the slope when I came up over a hill and misplaced the ground. Those three minutes of downhill training Val had given me were no match for the banana-peel ride ahead of me on my first mogul.

My poles made the sign of the cross as my butt skidded

downhill at lightning speed. Unfortunately, that part of my anatomy was unable to form a snowplow. But within seconds my legs reunited with my torso as I slid to a stop.

Encrusted in snow and grinning from ear to ear, I couldn't wait to get up and try again. Again and again I headed down that mountain until I was transformed into that rarest of beings: a downhill racer from the suburbs of Cleveland.

Skiing wasn't just a cool thing I did on weekends—it was freedom for my soul. Instead of hanging out in the lodge, I skied every available second. I didn't have much money, so I purchased used equipment and bought lift tickets from people who were leaving early. When the season ended on March 15, I was still trying to squeeze one more run out of the muddy, melting slope.

It wasn't long before skiing rivaled football as my favorite sport. Although I'd been a steady player at St. Michael's since the second grade, I'd just played my first football season at a "real" high school. The Catholic school always put out a lot of money for their sports programs, so I was used to first-class uniforms and fancy helmets. But the ninth graders at Independence High School were considered no more than a farm team for junior varsity. We played on a practice field, and no one even came to our games. I felt like I'd just transferred from West Point into a mercenary army. The glamour was gone.

Yet when I rode the bus to my first game that fall of ninth grade, I got the excitement to play again. As the coach made his way down the narrow aisle, I noticed he was looking right at me. Then he put his hand on my shoulder in a fatherly fashion, leaned down, and said, "Robinson, we're short of players. I need you to play guard today."

I was stunned. I'd always been the running back at St. Michael's, and now he was changing my position one hour before the first game!

"But Coach, I've never played that position. I've gotta be a back or a receiver."

"We're not out here for personal glory, Robinson. We're out here to win. If you can't get with the program, you shouldn't play on this team."

"Yes, Coach," I muttered, feeling like a man without a country. I felt totally overlooked and out of place for the first time in my sporting life.

I was switched to linebacker in the tenth grade, playing both sides of the ball. But changing positions didn't give me the recognition I'd had in the eighth grade. Some of the childhood thrill was definitely gone, as well as the Catholic school innocence.

"Blackie, fill in that hole," yelled one coach while smacking me on the helmet. "This line is leakin' like a sieve!"

They called me Blackie because I had a dark complexion and a heavy suntan, but I didn't really care what they called me. Oblivious that it was a racial slur and a putdown, I just wanted to prove I belonged. However, that desire took a hit when I messed up and the coach screamed, "Robinson! Out! *Again!*"

That remark burned me for years to come. I was giving football my best shot, but it didn't seem to matter. The coaches had their definite favorites, and I was going to have to just stick it out.

Activities had always been my means of soul expression, but now I was frustrated. Skiing was a definite high, but football wasn't giving me much of a sense of accomplishment anymore.

The ski slopes were only open four months out of the year, so I had to supplement my thrill-seeking soul with a new fix. Since I'd always excelled in sports, I decided to try gymnastics. Since we had no official program, I'd just compete against myself.

There was no one in the gym during that first lunch hour when I threw a bunch of inner tubes on the floor, laid wrestling mats on top of them, and began to teach myself gymnastics. Day after day I worked out on the high bar, parallel bar and flying rings, doing inlocates, dislocates, cutaways, and flips in the air.

I taught myself gymnastics from reading about it in books and using the equipment at school, but I wasn't trying to earn a letter or win some championship. I was doing it for the pure joy of movement. I learned the basics, then gravitated to the more advanced moves, pushing myself to the limit. When it came time to break a record on push-ups or squat-thrusts, I always rose to the occasion.

Before long I became the first kid at Independence High School to do a giant swing on the high bar. But that still wasn't enough to satisfy me. No matter how fast or how perfectly I moved, it was never enough. I felt increasingly distracted and could no longer find the release I craved. I was hungry—but for what?

Five

Somebody to Love

A re you bored, Mr. Robinson?"
Mrs. Mackey stood next to me in the aisle between desks in the classroom, her body language communicating polite disdain.

I looked up from my doodling and answered her honestly. "Yes, ma'am, I am."

"Well, I'm sorry to waste your precious time, Mickey. Would you please hand me that drawing you're holding? I'm going to get it analyzed, and maybe then we'll discover why you can't pay attention in class."

"If you find out," I said in all seriousness, "please let me know." My tenth-grade classmates snickered as Mrs. Mackey shot me the evil eye and walked back to her desk.

I wasn't a great student. Most of the teachers totally bored me, so I just drew pictures and got average grades. Yet for some reason, I got A's with demanding teachers and harder curriculum.

But being an average student didn't interfere with my social life. I was athletic, which naturally guaranteed me a space at the top of the teenage food chain. The winning combination was to be an athlete as well as being cool—then you were really a part of the right clique. During the mid-'60s, the popular mainstream emphasized looking good and feeling good. That's what made you popular, acceptable, and successful. There wasn't any emphasis on the more important values of *being* good and *doing* good.

46

The goals according to Mickey were pretty basic: I had to look good, stay excellent in sports, and meet the right girl. So far I'd aced the first two requirements for a happy life, but the girl of my dreams was still a phantom.

It certainly wasn't for lack of opportunity. I did more than my share of flirting and engaging in superficial relationships. I was a regular at all the neighborhood parties where the ultimate goal was to get the lights turned off so we could slow dance to Johnny Mathis and make out with someone.

Yet there was no one special in my life. Not until one winter night in 1965 when I arranged to meet a girl I knew at a party given by an old friend. Her name was Sue.

Stepping down into the concrete basement filled with bubble hairdos and mile-high stacks of Motown albums, I was ready for a good time.

"Hey Chuck, you seen Sue?"

"She's over there. Are you going out with her now, Mickey?"

"Nah. We're just friends. No big deal." Social, noncommittal relationship were pretty typical, and we had unwritten boundaries in our culture.

I spotted Sue and waved across the room. We gravitated toward each other, then joined the party scene.

Sue and I started doing our white, middle-class best to dance like we were from Detroit. Everything was fine until she got a little too much soul and accidentally flung her hand into a metal pole. When a herd of girls whisked her upstairs for an ice pack, I dutifully followed them to the kitchen. Fortunately the injury wasn't serious, but her hand was bruised. Her friends were taking care of her, so I left them alone.

As I walked back downstairs, I stopped on the steps for a minute and checked out the crowd. As my eyes locked onto the face of a petite and pretty brunette, everything suddenly froze.

Although I'd known this girl from St. Michael's, just then I felt like I was seeing her for the first time.

"Some Enchanted Evening" should have been playing as we drifted toward each other through the sea of madras shirts and mohair sweaters. Her brown eyes shone like melted Hershey's Kisses.

"Hi, Julie," I said to the girl of my dreams. "Long time no see."

She smiled. "I don't think I've talked to you since the eighth grade. It's good to see here."

"Wanna dance?"

"Sure, I'd love to." She tilted her head with a twinkle in her eye.

While we danced, I knew this was a totally different type of attraction than I'd ever felt before. I immediately replaced Sue of the Swollen Hand, and I didn't look at another girl the rest of the night.

When it was time to go, I lightly touched the tip of Julie's nose with my forefinger and whispered, "I'll see you later."

We stood there burning our initials into each other's eyeballs while waiting for the room to stop spinning. When she finally drifted out the door, I stumbled to the backyard for a cigarette with my old friend Chuck. Grinning like a Cheshire cat while blowing smoke rings at the moon, I pulled out the Standing Liberty silver dollar I'd carried in my pocket since I was seven years old.

"Here you go, Chuck," I said, casually flipping him my good-luck piece. "You can have this. I don't need it anymore."

I didn't need luck now that I had connected with Julie. She'd just filled in the last blank in my formula for happiness.

I proceeded to fall into the mystery and beauty of "the first love relationship." We became inseparable. Even though she was a junior and I a sophomore, we leaned against lockers and stared deep into each other's eyes for the next two years. After school we talked on the phone until we ran out of words, then just breathed meaningfully into the receiver.

We dated each other exclusively. The custom of going steady

included swapping our school rings—hers got jammed onto my pinky and my ring had to be wrapped in yarn to fit her left ring finger.

I was pleased and honored to be with Julie. She had many good qualities and was beautiful inside and out. Even though she and I did our share of steaming up car windows at Garfield Park, we never crossed certain lines.

The sexual revolution hadn't quite made it to Cleveland, probably because the Midwest is often last to join the party that moves from coast to coast. Whatever the reason, something always stopped us from going too far.

Still, we had a few struggles. After one argument, she gave me back my class ring. I frantically sliced the layers of yarn off the band. My confidence disappeared as I imagined breaking with her for good. She mattered to me more than I was willing to admit or even understood.

Luckily, our split lasted only twenty-four hours. Although we made up the next day, I still felt dissatisfied. What I needed from Julie was guaranteed, unconditional, nonrefundable love, and what I really wanted was for her to be something more than she was able to be. The void in me was beyond human relationship, but I didn't know what that was at that time.

Both of my sisters married right out of high school, probably in an effort to escape the drama of family trauma. My brother and I still lived at home with an alcoholic father and a mother who was frantically trying to hold everything together. The fighting got worse and more frequent. Mom seemed to try to do her part to stabilize everyday life. She'd have been better off trying to straighten deck chairs on the *Titanic*. My family was going down fast in a sea of anger, alcohol, and pain.

One night while on the phone with Julie, I heard the familiar sound of fighting coming from the kitchen. I hung up and walked directly into my father's line of fire. He looked at me coldly and said, "You still on the phone with that b----?" Then he stabbed a cooking knife into the breadboard.

Those words shot through me like poison, and suddenly I was acting out the nightmares I'd had of my drunken father and me. Without thinking, I shoved him up against the wall.

"Mickey, don't," my mother pleaded. "He's drunk! He doesn't know what he's saying. Leave him alone!"

But I could barely hear her as the emotions in me exploded from anger to rage. Memories clenched tightly in my fist, I punched him hard right in the face, knocking him across the room.

I know now that my dad would never have done anything to physically harm Mom. The appearance of that was an excuse for me to vent unrestrained anger.

Backing away from this broken man who was my father, I felt only disdain. As I banged the door open to storm out of the kitchen, I heard him mutter under his breath, "Thanks, Son."

The sound of his voice made my skin crawl. I couldn't stand to be around him or the atmosphere of the house. I moved to a friend's house for a couple of weeks to sort things out. When I returned home, my father wouldn't even look me in the eye. We never spoke about what happened, but simply swept the incident under the rug along with all the other broken days.

I hated this part of my life. I hated the way it made me feel. But I couldn't fix it and I couldn't make it go away. So I cast a magic circle around myself. The agonizing frustration of home couldn't touch me when I was inside my magic circle. Friends and sports and Julie became the safety zones I ran for in order to keep my sanity.

By my junior year, I just had to play football. I needed to pour myself into something. I attended all preseason workouts, spending hours working with weights and running drills for speed and endurance. Despite the sweltering summer heat, I found welcome relief in twice-a-day full-pad practices. I had never felt this kind of hunger and raw determination.

Every time I rammed my body into an opponent, I was dealing with something deep inside. The injustices of life became "the justice of sport."

The manager of the team noticed something had changed in me. He said, "Mickey Robinson is the hardest hitter we've got."

My name and number got announced over the loudspeaker pretty often that fall of 1966. I became adept at sacking the quarterback, and Independence High School had its best team record in twenty-three years. For the first time since those good old days at St. Michael's, it felt good to play football.

I didn't mind the grueling practice schedule, pushing my body past its limits, or getting up at sunrise day after day. When I stepped onto the playing field each Friday night, I entered into an arena that simply made sense. Give it all on every play; leave nothing on the field; no regrets. When I faced my opponent, I felt powerful enough to tackle a planet and wrestle it to the ground.

On opening kickoff I went into a zone, flowing with the one thing I was able to express—passion on the field. Real chemistry formed within our team, and I was making a significant contribution. It was fun to win week after week. Prior to then, we were usually listed in the paper as the underdog.

That fall of 1965, Julie was a senior and her name had been placed on the ballot for homecoming queen. She was selected as one of three attendants, but I sent her a dozen red roses with a note saying, *You'll always be my special queen.*

On a magnificent October afternoon, I got to stand on the sidelines in my uniform and watch Julie pass by in a white Mustang convertible at halftime. As I took off my helmet, the screaming fans cheered us.

The marching band screeched out a popular song as the current homecoming queen and her attendants rolled slowly by. As Julie turned to flash me a smile, her tiara sparkled in the gold autumn sun. She was beautiful, and she was my girl. I felt pretty cool.

That day seemed a good omen of our future together. The handsome football player would marry the pretty brunette, and we'd live prosperously ever after with our 2.2 athletically inclined children. Like a game show contestant on a winning streak, I assumed any door we opened would yield happiness. Little did I know what lay ahead of us, not too far up the road.

Six

Choices

A lump formed in my throat as I read the inscription on Julie's senior picture that spring of 1966: *Dear Mickey...If it's meant to be, it'll be.*

Leaning up against her hall locker, I asked, "Whaddya mean by that?"

"I mean we'll see what happens when I get back from Europe," Julie said matter-of-factly as she neatly stacked books on the shelf.

"Europe?"

"Yeah. Marlene and I are thinking about backpacking through Switzerland and France this summer. It's something we've always wanted to do."

"And what about me? What am I supposed to do while you're gone?"

"You'll be busy working and having fun. C'mon, Mickey, don't make such a big deal out of it!"

Everything seemed so easy for her. And why not? She was going to Europe and then on to college. I was looking forward to a sweltering summer job that was boring and menial. But there was nothing I could do about the injustice of the situation. I was committed to a certain lifestyle that was self-supporting yet not self-fulfilling.

As it turned out, Julie's big travel plans never materialized. She ended up spending the summer at home, packing boxes and talking about college. We did our regular see-you-every-day date routine. Every once in a while I got a weird feeling that her going to college would be a wedge in our relationship, but I'd quickly shake it off. Although we were headed in different directions, Julie was still my soul mate. Of that I was certain.

When the day finally arrived, I stood in her driveway, surrounded by piles of shoeboxes and suitcases. She left me with a kiss and promised to call me as soon as she got there. Julie jumped in the car and headed for southern Ohio to begin her freshman year at the university.

As she disappeared into the sunset, I braced myself for my final year of high school. I'd spent much of the last two years hanging out with Julie and our senior friends, so now I was having to say good-bye to all of them. Chuck was off to college, Mike was getting a job, Frank was getting married, and Dale was joining the army.

Lots of guys were headed to Southeast Asia, but the consequences of military service weren't real to me yet. Vietnam meant little more than camo-clad men in combat boots jumping out of helicopters on the six o'clock news. I couldn't imagine being in a war that looked like a badly edited TV show.

But Vietnam was like a leaky faucet that never got fixed, and it just continued to drip until the pipes finally burst and flooded the basement of America. Then everything started floating to the top.

Universities turned into walled cities overnight as protests ricocheted from coast to coast. The word *revolution* became part of the daily vocabulary, and there was a thin column of smoke on the horizon from all the blazing flags, burning bras, and smoldering draft cards. Times were definitely a-changin' everywhere.

Everywhere, that is, except in Independence, Ohio. Although we were beginning to hear wild rumors about jumping on a peace train, my high school was still chasing the caboose. The class of '67 wasn't allowed to wear jeans, tennis shoes, or long hair, so most of us looked like fugitives from the innocent TV show *Leave It to Beaver.*

This was the true weirdness of the '60s. An eighteen-year-old couldn't wear jeans to school in Ohio, but he could carry an M-16 to war in Vietnam. Something was definitely wrong with this picture, and as the war escalated and the messages in the music were social protests or psychedelic hypnosis, kids all around me began turning on and dropping out.

The music of the '60s wasn't just revolutionary; it was religious. Kids chanted lyrics the way priests chant prayer. My whole generation listened as songs poured into the air like invisible torpedoes and then exploded into bright fragments of social chaos.

Everyone had a personal anthem, and mine was by the group Jefferson Airplane. Something powerful grabbed me every time I heard Grace Slick sing about needing, wanting, and finding someone to love.

Julie's absence left a big hole in my life. She regularly sent me letters in her delicate penmanship, talking about her sorority friends, classes, and campus activities that didn't interest me. There was no way I could connect or celebrate her whole college scene. But I enjoyed getting the letters just to read her *I love you* at the end.

Although I still skied, partied, and played football, I was just killing time until graduation. I had no real career plans. But I did have three solid goals for the future: stay out of the army, make a lot of money, and have an exciting life. I didn't care what I did as long as it had nothing to do with Vietnam, boredom, or the middle class.

With Julie in college, I outgrew high school. I was in perpetual senior slump, just going through the motions. After football season ended, there was nothing to do except cruise until June and then grab my diploma.

One day my English teacher stopped me in the hall and said,

"Mickey, can you come by the classroom later? I have something for you."

Carla Nesbitt was my toughest teacher, but she was also my favorite. All the kids liked this "with it" lady who related to them as human beings and not just as student stats and S.A.T. scores. She was my speech teacher my junior year, and I excelled as an A student. Somehow she provoked me to work hard.

Maybe it was because of the theme paper I wrote on the subject "What Would You Do If You Had 24 Hours Left to Live?" Everyone expected me to write something off the wall. But the day I read the paper aloud in class, they were all shocked by my first sentence: "From the time a person is born, they begin to die."

Pausing a moment before reading on, I noticed guys fidgeting uncomfortably in their seats and a few girls rolling their eyes at each other.

"Don't you think that sounds a bit negative, Mickey?" Mrs. Nesbitt asked gently.

"But it's true, right?" I remarked, then went on reading. "If I had twenty-four hours to live, I'd want to spend it skiing down a mountain in Austria or running on a beach in Tahiti. But most of all, I'd want to make my mother smile."

I glanced at the teacher, who was looking at me intently. I think she saw something in me at that moment—something I didn't see in myself. From that day on, she became an ally. She was one of the few adults I trusted. Yet I didn't know what to expect as I walked into her classroom that spring afternoon.

"You wanted to see me?"

Handing me a copy of *The Diary of Anne Frank*, she said, "I'm directing this play in April, and I want you to try out for one of the lead roles."

I was flattered, but I didn't let it show through my too-cool facade. "Sure, okay, I'll check it out."

"This is a very special play, Mickey," she said with seriousness. "Would you please read it over the weekend? I want you to try your hand at acting. I think you're a natural."

When I read that play and met the character of Peter, I knew him. In an almost eerie way, I could tell what he was thinking. Peter was a Jewish teenager trying to survive Nazi persecution in Holland, while I was a baby boomer trying to survive the '60s in America. We came from radically different worlds, yet our restlessness was the same.

Peter and I were both caged lions trying to break free of the family zoo. Peter was trapped in an attic in Holland with troubled family, and I was trapped in a house on Pleasant Valley Road that was anything but pleasant. I figured I could tell his story better than anyone else, so I confidently headed to the school auditorium on the day of tryouts. But as I walked toward the stage, everything got quiet. I could feel all eyes on me.

"Hey, Mickey, what're you doing here?" asked Lisa, a girl who sat behind me in English.

"I'm trying out for the play."

"No kidding! Wow. This is a really serious story. You think you can make it through the first act without laughing?" Her message was loud and clear: wise guys don't belong here. Rarely do teenage actors come from the ranks of people who are more physically expressive than artsy and emotional.

Everyone was surprised when I got the part, and I even heard rumors that Mrs. Nesbitt had only picked me because of my looks—typecasting, they called it. That remark stung me like a slap in the face, and I became determined to prove them all wrong.

Playing a character—stepping into someone else's head—was like entering a whole new world. Football was less of a challenge than what was happening on that stage.

In one of the scenes, I was supposed to run into my room and throw myself on the bed after being ridiculed by my father. As I did this, many people in the audience started to snicker and laugh, but something inside me shouted, *They're not getting it.*

I had to communicate the torment within this young man, so I jammed my face into the pillow and began to sob. Ad-libbing something that was not in the script. At that moment, the audience fell silent and several people started to cry. *Now they get it,* I thought. *Now they know what it's like to feel totally trapped.*

A strange peace flooded me. For the first time in my life, I felt like I wasn't just screaming into an abyss. Somebody was actually listening. I'd made an emotional connection. But it felt much bigger than that. It felt like I'd just discovered fire.

After Carla Nesbitt witnessed my amazing transformation, she began urging me to seriously consider a career in acting. Although I was flattered by the idea, I couldn't hold on to it. I had to live in the now, and right now my mind was consumed with Julie.

When Julie and I had a rare but intense argument, I needed to talk to someone. Carla Nesbitt was cool enough and willing to listen. But not even she understood the emotional importance of this relationship.

"I don't get it, Mickey. You're only seventeen. That's way too young to be getting serious. If I were you, I'd leave Ohio right after graduation and head for New York."

I had received an acting award in a statewide competition, so Mrs. Nesbitt assumed I could confidently skate my way into a career. But I still had this gnawing insecurity that never went away, like a boogeyman that had stalked me since childhood. It would disappear when I was doing sports or hanging out with friends. Outwardly I was confident, independent, even cocky. But inwardly there was a shadow of emptiness I was trying to fill with my natural abilities and temporary circumstances.

The only way I could keep it away was to stay busy and surround myself with people. I needed someone to hold back the loneliness, so I drank activity the way my father drank vodka.

"You don't understand. Julie is the most important thing in my life. I'm not going anywhere without her."

She looked at me the way most adults look at love-struck teenagers—like they've forgotten what it's like to feel passionate about anything.

"Okay. But I think you're wasting a good opportunity. Take my word for it, Mickey. The older you get, the harder it gets." She was trying to steer me clear of an emotional pothole, but I didn't heed the warning.

After the play was over, Mrs. Nesbitt stopped talking about my acting career. She politely let go of my destiny, and high school settled once more into a boring routine.

I somehow made it through until June, but just a few days before graduation, my guidance counselor called me in for a final interview. "What are your plans, Mickey?"

"I don't know. Maybe I'll get my old job back. I made a lot of money last summer. I'll be fine with that." I gave Mrs. Patterson a winning smile. "At least until something better comes along."

"Aren't you at all concerned about the draft?"

"No. I'm not going to Vietnam."

"Well, I wish you luck," she said, giving me that "poor dumb kid" look. "I hope everything works out for you, Mickey. But sometimes—"

"I appreciate your concern," I said, standing. I could tell she was revving up for a lecture on responsibility, so I politely excused myself and walked out of the office. I wasn't worried about my future. I knew something would come along.

And I was right.

Seven

Wall Street

The day before graduation, I checked the classifieds and spotted a job opening at a brokerage firm in Cleveland. Sitting there with newspaper in hand, I fantasized about little men in white shirts shouting and waving papers as buzzers and horns blared in the distance. It was a football scrimmage without helmets—the perfect job for someone like me.

I immediately put on my checkered sport coat and drove downtown to let them know it was me they were looking for. Walking confidently into that personnel office, I felt like Zorro on his way to fencing lessons.

After filling out the application and handing it back to the secretary, I asked, "Have many other people applied for this position?"

She smiled. "About three hundred so far."

I didn't feel like Zorro anymore. I walked out of that office with few expectations. I was only seventeen and had no experience, so I figured my chances were almost nil. But surprisingly, they called me back for an interview.

As I sat across the desk from the company's personnel director, I tried to look like I knew what I was doing.

"So, Mickey, tell me why you want this job."

"Well, sir, what you need to know about me is that I'm always where the action is. I'm up for any challenge, and I don't care how long the hours are."

Even though I was young and inexperienced, I exuded confidence. I was highly motivated and I really wanted in. If looks could get me into that brokerage firm, I knew I could dazzle them with charm and energy.

After the interview, the personnel director walked me to the door and then abruptly turned to shake my hand. "Congratulations, Mickey. You start Monday."

I wanted to pass out cigars, but I swallowed my enthusiasm and calmly answered, "Thank you." All the way home I saw myself in this flashy, ultramodern office like a first-round draft pick getting to be a starter!

When I finally jumped out of the car and burst through our front door, I couldn't hold it in any longer. Intoxicated with my own success, I shouted, "Mom I'm in! I'm gonna be a Wall Street wonder boy!"

The stock market was at flood stage as I took my first steps into the hit-the-ground-running world of high finance. I started on my eighteenth birthday. At first I worked in the back office, learning the business by being the final confirmation of all the daily trades. After a short period of time, a job opened up in the trading department of our firm. This was the company's hotspot, where all the action was generated. They sat me down at a table with five other people and gave me two phones, a headset, a yellow legal pad, and very simple instructions: buy low and sell high.

My job was specialized in making the markets and trading over-the-counter stock, and that's basically all I did eight hours a day. It was also my responsibly to set the price value of about forty companies our firm underwrote. It was a rare moment when I wasn't on both phones, taking orders and translating them into sales as fast as I could. There was so much frantic energy in that office, when the bell rang in New York, it was like thoroughbreds plunging through the gates at the Kentucky Derby.

I watched fortunes being leveraged on a daily basis, but it wasn't the money that turned me on. It was the action. We were riding a roller coaster that either climbed to the stars or derailed on the curve. I surrounded myself with hard-driving people who wanted more, and it felt glamorous.

My aggressive young boss sat only a few feet from me, swigging from a bottle of Maalox, smoking cigarettes, and talking on two phones. This guy was a millionaire at age twenty-nine, so I decided to watch every move he made.

Primed and ready for war first thing every morning, he approached the starting gate by saying, "Okay, you guys, we're gonna get 'em today. Put on your game faces and let's go!" The concept of mentoring wasn't in vogue then, but I couldn't find a hotter man to be trained by than him.

There was no time to get warmed up. We had to be hot when the bell rang and stay hot on adrenaline, donuts, coffee, and profit. Sitting there, surrounded by ringing phones and sweating coworkers, I felt like a dispatcher on D-day. My job was one long jolt from start to finish.

Everything amazed me. This was the first time I'd ever seen anything digital, and right in the middle of our office sat a Xerox machine as big as a car. Everything looked state-of-the-art, or at least I thought so, until the day a manager showed up to plug us into the brave new world.

As he installed what came to be known as *the system,* I watched spellbound. Computer technology hadn't yet made it to the brokerage houses of Cleveland, so this looked to me like something out of a James Bond movie. The installer didn't say much, but on his way out he left us with a parting word of wisdom: "People can fail, but the system can't fail."

No one spoke, but we all looked at one another as if we'd just heard from God. I was still pondering the enormity of his parting remark when the firm's vice president called me into his office.

"Mickey, I've got some cash, checks, and negotiable stocks to go to National City Bank right away. Can you take them for me?"

"Sure, no problem."

The bank was only a few blocks away, and since it was a mild September day, I decided to walk. As I grabbed the briefcase and started out the door, he laughed and said, "Hey, be careful! You've got half a million dollars in there!"

Our office was right in the center of downtown Cleveland, so the sidewalks were packed with people. As I threaded my way through the crowd, I felt more and more like a big shot. It's amazing what carrying half a million dollars will do for your ego.

Nobody has any idea what I've got in here. I tightened my grip and looked straight ahead.

When I walked into the bank, they politely escorted me to an office on the second floor. It was the most elaborately furnished business room I've ever seen. As I sat there waiting for some VIP to show up, I felt genuinely important for the first time in my life. I was being groomed to be somebody.

Shortly after that, I started carpooling with one of the accountants from the back offices. As we glided through the streets of Cleveland, he grilled me with a white-collar version of *Twenty Questions.*

"So, Mickey, how much money do you want to make?"

I felt like saying, "That's kind of a stupid question, isn't it?" But I restrained myself. This guy was serious, so I played along. "Uh…as much as I can!"

"Are you planning a long-term career in the market?"

"Yeah. I like the speed. I think I can go places as a trader."

"Some of us are taking evening classes at Cleveland State University. Are you interested in getting more education?"

Now I wanted to cuff the guy on the head and say, "Mellow out, will ya?" But Brian was one of those guys who set and pursued long-term goals. I, on the other hand, couldn't get that excited about climbing the corporate ladder. Although I wanted to make money and be somebody in the business world, this was all new to me.

But I was definitely enjoying the prestige of my job. All of a sudden, powerful businessmen in three-piece suits were taking me to lunch at the Pewter Mug. My previous experience of sit-down dining was limited to Sunday lunch with my family at a little Italian restaurant, so this was a whole new ballgame.

During my first lunch with "the boys," I tried to look sophisticated while everyone ordered stuff I'd never heard of before. I decided on the chef salad because it sounded like something a stockbroker would eat.

"What would you like for lunch, sir?" said an amazingly soft voice.

When I looked up from the menu, I saw an awesome-looking waitress in a leather miniskirt. She smiled. I smiled back.

"She's waiting for your order, Mickey," said one of the guys.

"Oh yeah, I'll have a chef salad."

"And what would you like to drink with that, sir?"

I'd just seen the movie *Goldfinger,* and I remembered James Bond's drink of choice. There was one little problem: I was eighteen, and the drinking age in Ohio was twenty-one. Yet I was sure everyone thought I was older. No eighteen-year-old would be hanging out with such important business types. It was worth a try.

"A martini, please." I had no idea what I was ordering, but it had to be incredible because James Bond drank it.

"Vodka or gin?"

"Pardon me?"

She smiled knowingly. "Would you like that martini made with vodka or gin?"

My dad always drank vodka, so I ordered gin.

When the waitress placed a very cool-looking drink in front of me a few moments later, I instinctively grabbed it and gulped. Trying to remain calm, I fought the immediate impulse to wash my mouth out with beer. Instead, I inhaled a forkful of salad while mentally placing martinis on my list of untouchable substances. They ranked right up there with liver.

But martinis and power lunches were only part of my initiation into the mysteries of the city. Culture shock really hit when I encountered the fast-moving women known as *city girls*. There were a lot of them in my office, and they were fast and more sophisticated than my friends from the suburbs.

One balmy summer night, six of them took me to a Johnny Mathis concert at the Music Carnival. We all sat around a table in a huge circus tent with the sides rolled up, while I turned up the charm in order to impress my one-night harem.

When the lights dimmed, a silver ball twirled overhead and tiny stars danced on the ceiling. As Johnny sang his velvet version of "Eleanor Rigby," one lovely young lady reached under the table and slid her hand gently into mine. It felt like high school.

We all went to her house for a nightcap afterward, but for some reason, everyone took off and left me sitting all alone. The next thing I knew, my hostess strolled out of the bedroom in her robe, sat beside me, pressed a drink into my hand, and invited me to stay awhile.

"Uh, no thanks. It's really late, and I've gotta get home." I'd had a fun evening flirting with the girls, but I had no intention of spending the night. Maybe it was because I had to work early the next morning, or maybe it was because of my Midwest small-town upbringing. Most likely it had to do with Julie. I'd really been missing her.

Much to the young lady's surprise, I got up and left.

Shortly after, I planned a trip to Julie's university for the big homecoming game. She made plans for me to stay at a fraternity house, and I couldn't wait to meet all of her friends and impress them with my corporate status.

"Hey, Nathan, this is Mickey," Julie announced as we walked up to one of the frat house inmates. "You know, the guy I told you about? The one who works for a stockbroker in Cleveland?"

From the guy's deadpan expression, Julie might as well have said, "He picks up horse manure after parades." He didn't even extend his hand, but sized me up with one glance before turning his attention back to Julie.

I got this same cool response from all of the frat guys. It didn't take long for me to realize that these collegiate types are only impressed by other collegiate types. My position in the stock market was of little or no interest. The frat boys seemed like a bunch of spoiled brats who were stuck up.

I didn't let it bother me. After all, I hadn't come to make friends; I came to see Julie and the big game and to have a good time.

That Saturday morning we shoved our way into the packed bleachers, hugging, laughing, and enjoying the crisp autumn air. Trumpets blared, drums pounded, and cheerleaders flipped as Julie cuddled next to me to keep warm. This was one of those days when it felt good to be alive.

Her university was playing Bowling Green, and whenever her school scored, I screamed my head off. This wasn't my school, but it was Julie's, and that was reason enough to jump up and down and shake my fist at the opposing team. I drank some beer with my hot dogs, so by halftime my bladder was screaming for mercy. But when I stood up to walk to the bathroom, I heard a droning noise overhead.

I thought maybe it was just a beer buzz, but when I looked

up I spotted a plane circling the stadium. My wandering attention immediately focused when the side of the aircraft opened and miniature men began falling out in perfect synchronization.

I heard a faint *whoosh* as members of the US Army Parachute Team tore through the atmosphere. Puffs of black-and-gold parachutes burst above them in the sky, and they drifted to earth like leaves in a summer breeze. When one of the skydivers floated directly over where I was sitting, my eyes followed him down to a perfect precision landing on the fifty-yard line.

At that second I made a silent vow to do that myself someday.

I'd read somewhere, "A man who makes a vow makes an appointment with himself at some distant time or place." On that day, I made an appointment to meet myself in the sky. When the exhibition was over and the band started to play, I whispered, "I'm gonna do that."

"What'd you say,?" Although Julie had been sitting next to me the whole time, I'd forgotten all about her. I was totally focused on the sight of those black-and-gold parachutes.

"Uh, hello? Earth to Mickey!" Julie laughed as she rapped me on the head with her knuckle.

I smiled at her numbly, still lost in thought. Something that would change my life forever had just passed before my eyes, but I couldn't talk about it. Sacred things disappear when you try to explain them, so I just tucked the moment away and wandered off to the bathroom.

Eight

Snap Decisions

An old friend was waiting for me when I arrived home after work on Monday. I'd known Danny since the first grade at St. Michael's, where he single-handedly convinced several of the nuns to reconsider their vocation.

"What kind of a job do you have that you dress like that?"

"I'm working at a stock brokerage firm in downtown Cleveland, a really good one."

He actually looked envious. "You think you could get me in?"

The question made me feel awkward, because I wouldn't feel comfortable trying to introduce him to my firm. I told him I would ask my friend at Merrill Lynch if there were any openings there.

Danny could be described as my worst best friend. He had all the right stuff but used it in all the wrong ways. Good looks, nice house, latest clothes, plenty of money, but he made recklessly bad choices. In a word, he was a playboy. He had just returned from spending time in California, where he experienced "the summer of love."

Danny landed an entry-level job in the back office of Merrill Lynch, then bought some business suits, ties, and a brand-new sports car to pump up the image. As it turned out, Danny liked happy hour more than he did the work hours.

After several consecutive nights out after work with him at

some of the swankiest places in town, I woke up. Squinting in the mirror I said, "I don't look so happy." I squeezed solution onto my contact lenses and said to my reflection, "I have got to get focused."

The summer of 1967 would go down in my personal history as the beginning of a radical departure of certain things that had been considered normal for me. The shift started when a small group of guys I knew decided to experiment with marijuana. We were so afraid of getting caught, we first tried it in the woods where we used to play as kids. Like a tribal ritual, using grass and listening to pop music seemed to expand our minds. It also numbed our common sense into believing "If it feels good, do it."

Danny became the resident expert in our group. Having spent time in California, he had already stepped across many lines into "the brave new world." The messages in all the songs we listened to were like permission slips to experiment with our lives, opening doors of perception to journey into Wonderland.

Playing contemporary urban corporate climber by day and cosmic adventurer on the weekends started to affect my work and my personal values. But the changes went unnoticed as I gradually adapted to sensual things, which can be very deceptive. Self-deception is the worst kind. You just don't see it coming.

The stock market was soaring, so time flew quickly during the day. Work was demanding yet energizing, literally a winner-takes-all type of rush. In the evenings, I listened to Danny brag about California in a haze of smoke blended with hypnotic, psychedelic music.

Julie returned from the university for the Christmas holiday. My office had a Christmas party at the nicest hotel in downtown Cleveland. She fit right in with my office friends and the lifestyle we were planning for the future. It was a great Christmas, and I got her a beautiful piece of jewelry that really impressed her father. Then she went back to the university and I went back to the brokerage firm.

Danny invited me over to his house one night right after the holidays. After an hour of smoking grass and making small talk, out of nowhere he blurted, "Man, I've been thinking you would really love California. You don't want to go through another dreary winter here in Cleveland, do you? There's no groove here. This town is years behind LA."

I didn't know how to respond, and the look on my face probably made my thoughts pretty obvious.

"You're just freaked about your job and your girlfriend. Come on, man. You're really good at what you do in business. You could cop a job easy in Southern Cal."

The marijuana effect had already hit the humor button. I laughingly said, "You are one far-out dude, Danny." I told him I needed to go home and get some sleep, flashing him the peace sign as I walked out the door.

In the following weeks he continued to bring up the move to LA every day after work, but I did my best not to think about it. There's something self-betraying about not trusting the courage of your own convictions.

One Friday, after weaving my way through the evening's rush-hour traffic, I had no sooner peeled off my suit and tie than I saw Denny's image in my bedroom window. "Wow, Danny, you kind of surprised me."

"Yeah, well, I'm full of surprises. Like are you ready to pack up and get out of here? We can be in Florida in twenty-four hours, on the beach and living the good life. You can have it all."

I spun around and looked right at him "Florida? Your entire rap has been all about California. What does this have to do with that?"

"Come on, brother. Throw on your coat and jump in my car. There's nobody home at my house." Danny's family was gone for the weekend. His parents had let him turn the basement of their home into an apartment that he called "the groovin' room."

He fired up a couple of T-bone steaks from his parents' freezer, served one to me with twelve-year-old scotch and a brass pipe full of private-stash weed. When it came to being persuasive, Danny probably could have sold brass knuckles to Mahatma Gandhi!

In this grand presentation, he told tell me that all the same things were happening in south Florida that were going on in California. When I asked him about his job at Merrill Lynch, he said, "Man, we can get the same jobs down there that we've got in Cleveland, except we'll have our own pad and everything that goes with it."

What he neglected to tell me was that he had been fired for being late to work so many times.

Till long past midnight, Danny paced the room, describing what it would be like to live by the beach and do whatever we wanted to do. There was something craftily charming about Danny. He was enticing me into living independently, free from a good job but also a very unpleasant life at home. Through the thick smoke I could almost see the sun getting brighter on the beach in Florida.

"Yeah, maybe you're right. We can have it all. But I have to give my boss at least two weeks' notice."

"No way. You don't owe those people anything. We're going to Florida, buddy!"

We spent Saturday sorting out our personal items to see what would fit in his shiny new sports car. Sunday morning we took off, heading south in a blaze of irresponsibility. Danny agreed to stop at Julie's university on the way so I could tell her about our big plans of southern comfort.

I thought she might be mad at me. Instead she seemed unusually attentive, and very quiet. She didn't try to talk me out of anything. Just asked, "What are you planning to do down there, Mickey?"

"I figure I'll check out all the brokerage firms in Fort Lauderdale. You know I've always been able to get a good job."

We walked around her picturesque campus holding hands. Back at her dorm, she told me that during spring break she'd come spend time with us in Florida.

I was feeling our emotions getting pretty thick, so I verbally changed the pace. "Hey, Julie, I'll call you every day, just like always." It was my way of reassuring her that nothing would change.

After a lot of really good kissing mingled with "I love yous," I said, "I've got to go now. It's just a couple of months until spring break." I walked about ten feet, then turned around with my reassuring smile. "I'll keep track of the days." The unresolved good-bye felt similar to what I experienced when I looked at my office door for the last time, knowing I was walking out of a very committed part of my life.

Danny and I drove into Fort Lauderdale with the top down and stylish sunglasses in place. Palm trees lined the streets filled with suntanned bodies cruising the sidewalks and lounging on the beach. It was a far cry from the gray streets of Ohio with its dirty snow and freezing temperatures.

We knew one person in the city. He was from our old neighborhood in Independence, Ohio, and he was an amazingly skilled guitar player. He worked in a club playing music. The club's owner owned numerous apartments, so we moved into a furnished apartment just a few blocks from the main road leading to the beach.

At first, Fort Lauderdale seemed like a glistening endless Friday night—everybody in tropical clothes drinking tropical drinks and looking for a good time. Sunrise and sunset became one big blur. I started feeling homesick for Monday mornings.

I made a weak attempt to get a job at a stock brokerage firm.

But in the South, being good wasn't enough; you had to know somebody. Even if I'd had a connection, it wouldn't have mattered. I had lost my confidence.

After only a few weeks in Florida, I realized I'd made the biggest mistake of my life. I felt sick inside, yet I couldn't roll back time. Somehow I had to work this out.

Danny was content to sleep all day and party all night, but I stopped going out with him to enjoy the nightlife. I landed a sales job in a retail store just to keep up expenses to live in a place that was no longer the Promised Land. I was more than a little embarrassed at what I'd done and started anxiously looking for a way out.

My answer came unexpectedly in the form of Jack Reynolds, a friend of Danny's who flew to Florida for a week of serious hedonism. Jack never stopped talking about his adventures, how fast he could make money, how easily he could pick up girls, and how he made money on the black market selling sporting equipment, jewelry, and anything else he could turn over. He was a worldly-wise hustler, and his stories made my head spin. But one night he said something that really got my attention.

"Hey, Mickey, an old lady from Canada is paying me to drive her Cadillac from here to Toronto. You want to come along and help me drive? I'll give you half the money."

That was it. The moment I'd been waiting for to escape from Sunrise Boulevard.

"I'll do it." I said resolutely. "When do we leave?"

I felt Danny glaring at me. I hadn't told him how much I hated being in Florida. I knew he wouldn't understand why I wanted to leave his fantasy world.

"What's the matter with you, Mickey?" Danny snarled with a sharp tone in his voice. "We just got here! You can't do this to me."

I looked him straight in the eyes. "This is your scene, not mine. No hard feelings, okay? I just gotta get out of this place."

Danny stopped talking to me. But I didn't care. I'd been in Florida for six weeks, and that was five weeks too long as far as I was concerned.

It felt good to break free of Danny's influence and do what I knew was right. I was being honest with myself and taking action to change my wrong direction.

Jack Reynolds went to get the car. By the time he brought it back, I had my stuff packed up, in spite of the icy atmosphere in the apartment.

The only thing faster than Jack's nonstop stories was the speedometer! While I listened with one ear to Jack's colorful misadventures, the other ear kept waiting for the sound of a police siren. The slowest we went was ninety miles an hour, and we only stopped for gas and bathroom breaks. Sleeping was not factored in to this fast and furious road trip. We lived on coffee, Coke, and candy bars.

One thing he said really got my attention. He talked about a job at a gas-appliance company in Cleveland that was going to open their spring season soon. The job was installing outside appliances at residential homes. The company supplied the sales and equipment, and the faster you worked, the more money you made, including bonuses.

"Sound good to you?" he asked, grinning like an army recruiter.

I had no money and needed to work. Of course it sounded good. I could hardly wait to get back home to Cleveland.

I'm sure we set the all-time Eastern Seaboard speed record from Florida to Canada.

After dropping the car off at this nice old lady's place in Toronto, I took my share of the expense money and jumped on an airplane back to Cleveland. The blinding March snowstorm we flew into seemed like an appropriate end to my disastrous misadventure. I had nothing with me except summer clothes. Talk about a cool reception! I felt like a man who just been paroled from prison. At least I had somewhere to go.

It was good to be home and see my own room in our familiar neighborhood. After my first sigh of relief, I listened to my brother Robbie tell me how bad things had been. "Dad's drinking got really bad. He started going to AA meetings every day, and Mom goes with him."

"You think it's helping?"

"I don't know. It's too soon to tell. He's trying, though, so I guess that's better than nothing."

Robbie was only fourteen, and he'd seen the worst of our domestic trauma. But he was very grown up for someone that young.

When my parents came home, they didn't ask much about Florida and I didn't volunteer any details. They were preoccupied with their own troubles.

Mom tried desperately to help Dad stay sober. But after six weeks, he fell off the wagon and started drinking early in the morning. It wasn't very long before Mom's endurance came to an end. After twenty-three years, she filed for divorce. My father left our house. My mother, after being a devoted, efficient, full-time mom and homemaker, went to work in a restaurant. I took Jack's advice and got hired at the gas-appliance company.

After basking in the glow of the stock market, this was a humiliating experience. There was no charisma. No prestige. No power lunches. No challenge, no satisfaction. I felt like I'd blown my big chance in the business world. I was holding down a job anyone could do.

Danny and the changing culture had been a bad influence on me, but I'd made my own choices. I had no excuse. But I was still searching. And as always, I was sure something better would come along sooner or later.

I probably wasn't home twenty-four hours before everyone knew I was back in town. A few of the guys from our secret society of marijuana users invited me to "put a good buzz on." As always it was accompanied with a mixture of psychedelic/pop music with anti-war, anti-materialism, anti-government, revolutionary lyrics like "Turn on, tune in, and drop out." I didn't quite get it, but it came with the package.

Cleveland, Ohio, the birthplace of rock 'n' roll, was about to host a major music event: The Jimi Hendrix Experience. The concert was a sellout, but I knew somebody at a local TV station who got me a center seat in the second row. All of the hippest music people in Cleveland were going to be there.

I had nothing resembling "freaky clothing" in my closet. I did have a long-sleeved pajama top that had purple blobs all over it. And a bear-claw necklace my sister got from her boyfriend. I had Beatles boots, And I wrapped a headband around my head of short hair. I looked like I was going trick-or-treating.

The concert hall was packed. As I squeezed through the entrance, there was an air of anticipation and excitement mixed with the smell of patchouli oil, jasmine, and whatever else the crowd had rubbed on their with-it clothes. They may have had the right clothes, but I had the great seats.

The curtain opened to reveal a wall of amplifiers and the three-piece band. Jimi Hendrix didn't say, "Good evening," or "Hi, how are you?" His greeting was unleashing the melody from his latest album with the song "Foxy Lady." The crowd roared with approval as he blasted out one song after another, improvising with searing guitar solos and sounds that had never been heard before.

He played guitar from behind his head, with his teeth, and finally on his knees, with squealing distortion and flashy finger work. As he ended with the song "Wild Thing," I got squashed to the front. Just a few feet away from the stage, I heard him mutter,

"Stoned, stoned." I was grossed out by his sexual antics with his guitar, but could not deny the hypnotizing power he had over the people.

The next day, the reviews in the paper quoted some people complaining about the rush to the stage. I thought, *He was begging for personal attention, and he had the power to influence.* The cover story on *Life* magazine called him a demigod. Today I would call it mob psychology.

That concert added to my conflict. All of the anthems were about peace and freedom, but after the smoke cleared, I didn't feel very peaceful and I certainly wasn't free. I was just searching for something to believe in.

Nine

Dream Catcher

One early spring day in 1968, I walked through the front door after work and heard my brother, Robert, tell me, "Mom wants you to look at the toilet. It isn't working." With Dad gone I had to pick up the slack.

Flipping through the Yellow Pages for plumbing parts, I stopped when I saw a listing for the Parachute Club of Medina. Momentarily forgetting the plumbing problem, I dialed the number.

"I'm interested in your classes on skydiving. How do I start?" There was a weird silence on the other end. I wondered if I'd been cut off.

Finally a voice answered, "There is no parachute training here right now. This is Freedom Field. We're offering a special five-dollar introduction on private flying lessons."

The field was only about twenty-five-minutes away, so I decided to drive over and check it out.

The place looked abandoned. But I'd driven all the way over, so I decided to take their five-dollar promotional flight. The cheap price was just a marketing hook, and in my case, it worked. After my introductory flight, I discovered that I had an aptitude for flying the little Cessna. The instructor commented that I had natural instinct and ability to fly. That day I signed up for flight lessons.

The first few flights were good, and learning to fly filled up some of the emptiness I felt after making bad decisions. I didn't know it then, but I was groping to repair my damaged identity.

A few days later I read an article about a man who'd invented a miniature helicopter kit called a Benson Gyrocopter. It had a VW motor, a wooden propeller on the back, and a tricycle gear for landing. With a helicopter blade on top and a seat made of tubular aluminum, it resembled a flying lawn chair. This mini helicopter had been featured in a James Bond movie. I was fascinated.

The article said the gyrocopter was currently on display at the Cleveland Sportsman's Show, so I hurried down to have a look.

I happily wandered around the show until one particular sign caught my eye through the colorful maze of booths. It said Cleveland School of Sport Parachuting, and below it a small crowd had gathered to watch a slide presentation of people in free fall. As I stepped closer to the awesome images, I heard someone ask, "Are you interested in skydiving?"

Standing behind the display counter was a man in a skydiver's jumpsuit with a big smile and a brochure in his hand. I could tell he was gearing up for the sales pitch, but I saved him the trouble by asking, "Where do I sign up?" I forgot all about the gyrocopter!

A few days later, I was on my way to an airfield in the beautiful Amish country about an hour from where I lived. I spotted a dirt runway with two Cessnas parked and an assortment of long metal buildings. I got out of the car, marched into the office, and announced, "I'm Mickey Robinson, and I'm jumping today."

For the next five hours, Lucy, my instructor, guided me up a stepladder and buckled me into a military T-10 harness suspended from the ceiling beam of the clubhouse. Even though it was basic stuff, I drank in every word, hanging there while she spieled out a brief overview of skydiving. I was far more attentive and diligent in following these instructions than I was at listening to airplane instructions.

Next she showed me how to pull up on the risers—the canvas straps that attach to the parachute lines. When a parachutist pulls down on one of the four risers, it curls and slightly pulls in that part of the parachute edge. When the parachute is fully inflated, the air escaping under it giving you some minimal ability to control or steer the parachute. This was a perfect chute for beginners, and they'd made its operation practically foolproof.

We spent most of the day repeating emergency procedures such as different types of malfunctions and reserve parachute deployments. I mastered all the techniques without a hitch.

The next part of the training was about how to land. They had me jump off a picnic table and do it PLF—parachute landing fall. Because of my gymnastics aptitude and strong legs, I nailed it perfectly the first time and every other time.

The last step was to simulate, while on the ground, exiting the aircraft. Completely outfitted with all the equipment, I stood on a step with one foot, both hands on the wing strut. At the instructor's command, I acted out a perfect execution of this training.

When it came time to jump out of the plane, I was told, my body weight would pull and extract the chute automatically. This jump was pretty much identical to the military maneuver called a static line jump. Even if I froze in midair, the chute would open.

As Lucy rattled on for three hours about various malfunctions and emergency procedures, I was excited about everything. I focused on the most important things: how to exit the plane and position myself to simulate free fall; counting to three and checking the opened parachute, and remembering the appropriate emergency procedures if the main parachute malfunctioned.

Wearing a motorcycle crash helmet and black goggles, I looked like a mutant fly as I hopped aboard the little Cessna 180. I shook hands with the pilot, Dale, then excitedly settled into my seat.

After climbing to 2,800 feet, Dale slowed the plane down to eighty miles per hour. He reached across my chest and said, "Now I'm gonna open the door."

I felt like a little kid being strapped into a roller coaster. Dale kept telling me everything he was doing so I wouldn't panic, but panic was the furthest thing from my mind.

As the door opened a half-mile above the earth, I felt a sweet, cool rush of heavenly wind. Unable to hear anything but the hypnotic drone of the engine, I gazed down at the amazing patchwork quilt of Amish countryside. It was the most beautiful sight I'd ever seen, and the smell of the air made it doubly intoxicating.

For a brief moment I was lost in space, but then I remembered I was supposed to jump out of the plane! I snapped back to attention, reached out the open door, grabbed hold of the wing strut, and pulled myself onto the welded steel step. I couldn't help but notice the wing strut was almost stripped of paint from all the scratch marks made by human fingernails. I guess a lot of people had a hard time letting go!

Dale alternately looked out his window and back at me to determine the exact spot for me to jump. As I waited for his signal, I held myself in perfect position, exactly as I was told.

When Dale finally found the spot, he slapped me on the leg and yelled, "Okay, go!"

As I pushed off, I put my arms and legs out, just the way I'd been taught. Instantly I heard an unfamiliar *whoooshhhh*. Then perfect silence.

The quiet was unbelievable. As the scenery whizzed past me like a speeding train, I tried to remember what I was supposed to do next.

Just then I felt a slow tug that set my body straight up. Instantly I was suspended beneath this olive-drab canopy, hanging quietly above the earth, suspended in the sound of silence. As I surveyed the earth from a half-mile up, I was overwhelmed. I felt like I was driving the winning chariot in *Ben-Hur*—except my horses weren't made of flesh and blood. They were made of air.

I noticed my feet floating freely above the beautiful green earth. Ohio looked perfect from up there, and no one was in a hurry. Cars and trucks and people were all moving at the humble speed of a snail.

Drifting in a sky-blue daydream, I momentarily forgot that I was falling to earth. But the instructors had planned for that. As I neared the hundred-acre field where I was to land, I heard a deep voice booming out of nowhere, filling the sky around me.

"Okay, Mickey, you're looking great. You're coming right in. Keep your eyes on the horizon."

They'd rigged up a PA system in order to remind first-timers that the ground was an essential part of the jump. In the last few seconds, beginners have a tendency to look down and pull their legs up. "Keep your eyes on the horizon, Mickey. Pull up on the risers, and get your feet together."

I obediently pulled my feet together, but couldn't resist looking down. The eternity of the sky instantly slammed shut as the ground came keenly into focus. Feeling a sharp jolt, I tumbled softly and it was over. In less than four and a half minutes, Ben-Hur disappeared and Mickey Robinson took his place. I felt joyful and exhilarated, and aggressively excited to do it again.

After a moment of congratulations from my instructor, everyone disappeared. To them this was business as usual, but I was lit up like a Roman candle. I dutifully followed Dale into the clubhouse to sign my name in the little logbook. It's customary for the pilot to sign off by marking the date, altitude, and a few comments about the jump. His comments read, "Perfectly executed."

I felt like a kid who's dying to ride the roller coaster one more time, but this was Dale's last load of the day. I could tell he was ready to head for home, yet he kindly took the time to offer me a shot of whiskey and a parting cigarette. As he signed off the paperwork, I asked, "What's next?"

He told me that most people make one jump and are never heard from again. Only one out of ten ever return for a second jump, and the ones who become skydivers are rarer still. But I knew, without a doubt, I was coming back.

"We've got this package deal," he explained. "You get seven jumps for $125.00, and by the sixth jump, you're in free fall if you do everything right. How does that sound?"

"Sign me up!"

On the way home I kept shouting, "Yes!" at the top of my lungs while honking the horn and picking up speed. I'd finally found it! Something was exploding inside me. Skydiving was incomparable to any other experience. It surpassed all of my former athletic accomplishments. It was better than my career options. Better than money. A much better high than marijuana and rock concerts.

Skydiving was the single most liberating thrill for me, and it provided a sense of freedom from the mundane and uninspiring daily circumstances my careless choices had created. And it added a sense of accomplishment and discovery. I felt like I was made for this sport. Skydiving was fine wine and I wanted to enjoy every bit of tasting it.

Not everyone shared the same enthusiasm I had for my newfound pleasure. After a while, my friends starting rolling their eyes and telling me to shut up. But that didn't faze me. I was a man with a vision! An uninspiring job and Julie's absence at college didn't bother me anymore. I was totally focused on skydiving and more passionate about it than anything I had ever been involved in.

I advanced rapidly through the first five jumps, and three weeks later I experienced my first free fall. I jumped from the plane, made a big X with my body, and immediately became stable. I felt like a leaf drifting down from a tree as I counted one thousand, two thousand, then pulled the ripcord on three thousand.

The brilliant red T-U parachute slid easily out of its pack, unlike the bulky T-10, and exploded above me. I was no longer restricted, but could now pull on the steering lines and actually maneuver in the sky.

That day I maneuvered myself a little too far out of the drop zone and landed in the woods. But I didn't care—any more than Lindbergh cared that he was a few miles off on his first transatlantic flight. After gathering the parachute into my arms, I sat silently on a log to savor the moment. I couldn't move. I was numb with peace. I'd just experienced baptism…breakaway… a true beginning! I was born for the sky, and I passionately embraced it—body, mind, soul, and spirit.

I immersed myself in the skydiving culture and became fluent in its language. Terms like *free fall, terminal velocity, relative work,* and *dead center* became part of my working vocabulary. All I ever thought about was skydiving. When I woke up in the morning and looked out the window, my first thought was *Is this a good day for a jump?*

Although my world was still mostly black and white, it turned a radiant Technicolor when I stepped onto that runway. Skydiving became the object of my full attention; everything else was just filling up space. Working at Gaslight was a means to an end; it provided money to support my compulsive habit and to pay bills, in that order.

Each day it seemed I had less in common with the guys I hung out with, especially Danny. He had returned from Florida and was still mad at me for leaving him there.

The final straw came on the morning of June 6, 1968, when my clock radio woke me up with a news bulletin. Robert F. Kennedy, leading front runner for the nomination to be president, had been assassinated in Los Angeles, California. I lay in my bed, looking at the ceiling, and felt sick to my stomach. *Not again.* Only two months had passed since the assassination of Dr. Martin Luther King, Jr. shocked the world, and only five years since John F. Kennedy was assassinated. I pulled myself together and dressed quickly, but could not stop thinking about the terrible loss of a promising, charismatic leader for our nation.

I arrived at work and was waiting in line to get my packet of job orders for that day when I overheard some of the workers joking about the assassination of Robert Kennedy. I was disgusted. Some of the employees were really low-life people, and I couldn't stand being around them anymore. So I quit.

I got my old job back at the Baker division of Otis Elevator. My new coworkers were friendly enough, but they couldn't relate to my obsession. When I tried to describe the wonders of free fall, I received everything from smiles to scorn.

"You think it's cool being a skydiver?"

"Sounds good, Mickey. I wish I could try something like that."

"I've got a wife and kids to support. I can't throw money away like you single guys."

It only cost me $3.50 a jump, but I was jumping as often as possible, so my bills were beginning to stack up. My worldly possessions consisted of a car, ski equipment, and clothes, but I didn't care about those things much anymore. All I wanted was my very own skydiving gear.

I heard about a skydiver from our club who'd recently decided to quit jumping, so I bought his equipment—including a red, white, and blue Para-Commander parachute. I ordered special boots and a white jumpsuit with elastic sewn around the wrists, neck, and ankles. Although I'd never placed much value on material possessions, these items quickly became sacred to me.

Purchasing my own gear was like receiving vestments for ordination. I was now able to participate in the ritual I loved above all else. I was ready to take my vows as a priest of the sky. My childhood dreams of flying like Superman, participating in the space program, and everything else above the earth, including the beauty of the clouds, got transformed into reality. I was like a caterpillar that had turned into a butterfly.

Ten

What Goes Up...

Oone rainy day I was in the clubhouse packing my parachute when a man I'd never seen before came strolling in. I couldn't take my eyes off of him as he walked up and tossed a flexible metal tube onto the table in front of me.

The tube held a parachute ripcord, and it had a little stone wedged just inside the opening. He flashed me a wry smile, pointed to it, and said, "If anybody asks, that's pea gravel."

He was referring to the ball-bearing-shaped stones that cover the small area skydivers call the ground target. He was telling me, "I always go for dead center," which is a six-inch-diameter disc—a skydiving bull's eye to target from over two miles high.

As I tried to think of an intelligent comeback, he turned and walked out the door.

"Who *is* that guy?" I asked.

"That's Dan," said a pilot standing nearby. "He's D-44." That meant he was the forty-forth person in the United States to qualify for the top license in skydiving.

"How come I've never seen him around the drop zone before?"

"He had a minor surgery, so he's been out for a while."

The pilot told me Dan had a reputation for being a gung-ho, purebred, totally sold-out skydiver. He was like a hard-nosed gunslinger who was never afraid of a challenge. If he made a commitment to do something, he would push the envelope to keep his word.

In conversations I overheard behind my back, I was being referred to as "the superstar" because of how quickly and proficiently I excelled in the sky. But when Dan looked at me, there was something compelling in his gaze. I didn't know it then, but he was testing me, checking me out. And I was intrigued by D-44.

From that day on, Dan became the man to watch. I thought of him as a skydiving legend who had the right stuff. But in daily regular life, he was a forty-something Irish Catholic who liked to drink whiskey.

While growing up in a tough Cleveland neighborhood, Dan had fallen in love with extreme challenge and it turned out to be a lifelong romance. Employed as an ironworker, Dan liked climbing to the top of skyscrapers and walking out on six-inch beams so he could catch a bird's-eye view of the city.

Although he swore like a sailor and drank like one, he never jumped out of an airplane without making the sign of the cross. He had a reverence toward God, but since he was divorced, he wasn't allowed to take communion. So for him Sunday was all about jumping.

Dan thrived on show jumps and relative work, but he wasn't a show-off. He just loved free fall.

In the makeup of committed skydivers, there were two separate groups. The first was the stylists, who competed in an individual free fall event requiring a series of maneuvers precisely executed and measured with a stopwatch. Our club had the best stylists in the world. The second group was jumpers, who liked to do relative work—high-level teamwork, forming snowflake-like formations at terminal velocity. It's called *relative* because each jumper needs to maneuver and adjust his aerial velocity to connect with all the others.

By this time, I was jumping at 7,500 feet, which gave me thirty seconds of free fall.

As I fell into that huge hammock of clouds, I instantly stretched and turned and made myself comfortable maneuvering in the sky. As I twisted and arched my body, I was elated to find I could zoom or track through the air two feet horizontally for every vertical foot I fell. When I flung my arms back and slightly spread my legs to engage in tracking, I could feel the acceleration as I moved horizontally. It was like I was flying.

With every jump, I became more sensitive to time and distance. My eyes let me know how far I was above the earth while my brain ticked off seconds as accurately as a Swiss watch. I knew not to trust altimeters and watches. All the best skydivers rely on an inner knowing of what to do and when to do it, and I was going to be one of the best.

As I got more comfortable with free fall, I couldn't wait to make contact in relative work. In this deceptively simple-looking maneuver, the first person out is called the pin man. He jumps and falls stable in a fixed position, then waits until the next skydiver can fly over, make contact, and then hook up.

The second jumper has to increase his speed at first and then slow down in order to mesh with the pin man. Although it looks easy, it's entirely possible for unskilled skydivers to overshoot or crash into each other. Although I tried it with a couple of different people, each time was a disappointment. We looked like kids trying to grab each other's butts rather than skilled skydivers trying to successfully execute a difficult and delicate maneuver.

After one botched attempt, Dan walked up to me and said, "I hear you're having a problem making contact."

"Well...yeah...I—"

"You wanna make contact?" he interrupted. "Come with me."

He didn't wait for an answer, but turned on his heel and walked into the clubhouse. I could hardly believe it. Dan was inviting me to jump with him. That was like Wyatt Earp asking me to be his deputy.

Dusk had begun to fall by the time Dan and I took off for our first jump together, but the sun had not yet set at ten thousand feet.

"I want you to fall stable and find something big to look at, like a barn or a pond," Dan explained as our plane climbed into the brilliant summer sky. "Keep your eye on that thing, make the biggest X you can, go as slow as you can, and wait. I'll be there."

I went off the step nearly two miles above the earth, fell in a perfect X, and then spotted a big white barn three or four miles away. Remembering Dan's advice, I aimed for it and didn't move even one degree to the right or left. With arms outstretched and hands cupped, I tried to grab as much air as I possibly could. Falling straight and slow, I heard the now familiar sound of my body ripping through the air...*shoo-whoosh.*

I felt a tug on my ankle. As my body spun sharply around, two strong hands grasped my wrists and pulled me to within eight inches of Dan's grinning face. At that moment, he welcomed me into the brotherhood of the sky. I was being initiated into a secret society, and it felt religious, like God touching Adam.

I was no longer alone with the clouds and the earth and the air. I had made contact with another human being. That changed everything. I suddenly understood why Dan loved relative work. Free fall was too awesome, too sacred, not to be shared.

As we neared opening altitude of two thousand feet, Dan and I pushed away from each other like separating spacecraft. I lifted my upper body to track in the opposite direction. When I was well away from Dan, I waved my arms above my head before pulling the ripcord. As the red Para-Commander billowed out, it jerked and spun me around just in time to catch Dan's last moment of free fall.

For a split second, it looked as if I went rocketing toward heaven while he continued hurtling toward earth. As the sky swallowed his solitary figure, I saw for the first time, from the sky, what a man looked like free falling at 125 miles per hour.

I saw a tiny poof as Dan's chute opened and he bobbed gently in the sky like a red lure on blue water. As I watched him from a distance, I felt elated. The connection was more than physical. He was giving me his best from skill and experience, and something of my best got activated!

The sky was a lot darker by the time we landed, and I was like a little kid on the Fourth of July. Aglow with elation, all I wanted to do was stay on track with this man and learn the tricks of the trade. I logged this jump with carefully defined black lettering: *10,000 feet-first contact in free fall,* signed *Dan Harding D-44.*

After tossing our gear into the back of the car, we drove up to a little country bar where skydivers relived their greatness jumps like soldiers fresh off the front line. After a few beers, Dan said. "Are you good to go tomorrow?"

"Oh, yeah."

Dan was inviting me into his inner circle! I drove back to the hanger to sleep on my silky open parachute, eager to be on the first lift the next morning.

Dan and I made many more jumps together, and ultimately he asked me to become a partner in his show jump demonstration team. This seemed like the coolest opportunity I'd ever received. Dan was a legendary maverick in the sport, and he was highly respected. This man had survived more than his share of bad landings, but nothing could keep him out of the sky for very long.

After Dan took me on as his partner, my star rose rapidly. The other competitive skydivers noticed my aerial abilities, and it wasn't long before I started getting offers to take part in show jumps for political functions and church carnivals—public appearances where we were the highlight entertainment for large gatherings.

After a successful demonstration jump, we would shake hands with the little boys and girls as they checked out our parachute gear—like public relations for the sport of skydiving and for our team specifically. As we strolled through the crowd, everyone wanted a smile, eye contact, and a wave. I sensed that we were giving them something new and exciting. I also noticed the girls checking me out with a little extra fascination. That wasn't hard to take, to say the least.

I belonged to the elite group of athletes who talked nonstop about attractive girls, free fall, competition, and themselves. I quickly learned there was a caste system to this sport, and its top gun was known as the national champion. Our club was home base for the most advanced skydivers in the USA, including him.

I also learned that most high-performance skydivers believed in little more than themselves. Some would even curse and mock God before jumping off the step. That part seemed strange to me. I just ignored it because I was so taken by the sport and its top guns. These were young, healthy, world-class athletes who lived on the edge and took pride in their excellence. Their religion was free fall and their altar was the sky. Beyond that, not much mattered.

But Dan was different. This man was no saint, but neither was he a blasphemer. Dan steadfastly believed there was a God to be reckoned with, and I liked that about him. Both of us were drifting from the church, yet we had been forever marked by the fear and wonder of a Catholic childhood.

One day, one of the country's best FL style jumpers walked up to me after a jump and said, "You really ought to consider style competition. All the guys have been watching you and they said you should enter the next competitive meet."

I recognized him as one of the elite and was flattered to be invited to join these ranks. Being new at this sport I was also naïve and had not picked up on the banter between the competitive stylists and the relative workers. I soon learned that I had to choose between one or the other.

With each jump I sharpened my skills at aerial maneuvers. It was obvious that I could excel at both of these skydiving competitions. But for some reason I was gravitating toward relative work and Dan Harding.

My other life, the one outside of skydiving, was divided in less important files marked *girlfriend*, *job*, *old friends*, and *faded glory*.

When Julie came back from school, she found out about my new lifestyle as a sport parachutist firsthand. She didn't fit into the skydiving scene, other than all the guys checking her out. They could tell she was pretty and classy. Once she rode up in the plane to see me jump from the top floor: 12,500 feet. I leaned back in the plane, gave her a really good kiss, and pushed off, waving as I speedily fell to the earth. The plane shrank from full size to a disappearing dot in a matter of seconds. I think she kind of enjoyed that, but everything was happening so fast we didn't talk much about my passion or my purpose in being a fanatic.

My job was tolerable. It brought in pretty good money that could buy me really great pleasure.

Danny was still bitter toward me for leaving him in Florida. We had never really resolved it, and I didn't much care; it was over as far as I was concerned. Some of my old friends were being introduced to experimenting with marijuana. But as the drug's effects began to sedate us, it became a ritual. It was always accompanied by the newest psychedelic music: Jimi Hendrix, Eric Clapton, Cream, The Doors, Jefferson Airplane. Their songs gave us permission to enter the forbidden zone of adjustable moral boundaries. They also opened up dialogues about all kinds of mystical parallels and secret meanings about peace, truth, even the meaning of life itself. The fact that marijuana smoking was illegal made us very cautious. In those days you had to be really careful about letting anyone know you were "turned on"—except for other users.

I never let this part of my life cross over into skydiving. I wanted to be completely alert and unaffected while even thinking about jumping. All of the skydivers made fun of potheads and college hippies. While among the skydivers I didn't think of myself as a pot smoker, but I did not feel like a hypocrite. I was a different person as a skydiver.

The other part of my life was far less important and growing dimmer. My old friends were the past, and I was only interested in the now, literally living for the moment—those pure seconds suspended in the rare air of free fall and eager to do it again.

Dan talked to a few of us about starting our own club closer to where we lived, and developing a new drop zone and training center for the more devoted skydivers. In addition to our demonstration team, we would make money by training our own students. A pilot who had flown us on a few successful show jumps close to the city of Cleveland was interested. We began jumping on a regular basis in a community south of Cleveland in Brunswick, Ohio, where he kept his planes.

We started offering to train students and were surprised that quite a few came out to our primitive, humble location for their first jump at The Brunswick Flying Ranch.

One of our first students was a sixteen-year-old female. Dan was her instructor, and she executed her first two jumps perfectly.

Under the watchful eye of her pretty, blonde mother, we went up for her third jump in a six-passenger low-wing Piper aircraft. All of the seats had been removed except the pilot's seat. I sat on the floor across from the open baggage door where the jumpers would be exiting. Dan had broken his thumb and had a cast on his right hand and wrist, so he wasn't jumping on this flight.

At 2,800 feet above ground, she was seated on the floor with her legs dangling out in midair and about to jump on Dan's command. I happened to notice that her static line—the opening apparatus— was stuck in the back of her parachute rigging. It was supposed to be clipped onto a metal hook on the inside of the aircraft! Before I could say anything, Dan shouted, "Go," and out she went.

Without thinking, I instinctively lunged out into open space, chasing her. She was already several hundred feet away from me and accelerating. I went into a head-down dive. She was waiting for the static line to open the parachute, and that wasn't going to happen. I envisioned myself getting to her, then slowing my speed to match her rate of descent—basically tackling her in midair and flying away with a reserve ripcord in my hand, saving her life.

As I closed in, she rolled over on her right side and I saw a white puff of the reserve canopy. I veered off and whizzed past her like a missile. I experienced for the first time what is called *ground rush*. Buildings grew in size like expanding balloons. My field of vision changed so rapidly it did a terrifying number on my brain's perception. In no more than a second or two, I pulled my main ripcord. The opening shock jarred my rib cage a little, but I was never happier to look up into an open parachute.

That little gal did what she was supposed to do perfectly, and we both landed safely. But she never came back. Even if she'd wanted to, I doubted her mom would allow it.

Dan thanked me for my valiant effort. Although it was his mistake, and a serious one, we never talked about it after that. Speaking about personal issues as being right or wrong would be like putting each other down, and there was an unspoken law in this sport of being positive, sure, and absolute.

Things had changed rapidly for me in a little over a year. I'd been focused on a long-term career, marriage, eventually a family, and a successful professional and social life. Through foolishness and careless decisions, I was now living for the moment, inhaling the power of personal gratification. Though people my age were disappearing to a savage war zone called Vietnam ten thousand miles away, I was oblivious to the possibility that I might be called at any moment. Not even when a buddy of mine was killed in action.

This young man had been one of the most fun-loving, charismatic guys at my high school. When he skipped college for one semester, he got drafted into the Marines. He wasn't in Vietnam for even a month when his life was snuffed out by a sniper's bullet.

I visited his final resting place with his closest friend, a highly decorated Special Forces soldier who'd also served in Vietnam and survived unbelievable combat situations.

We stared at the stone monument with the date of his birth and death—such a brief period of time. After a long, solemn moment, this friend told me about some of the horrors he'd witnessed.

The summer of 1968 would go down in history as a volatile, social convulsion all over the world. As real as this war was to these brave combat soldiers, it was unreal to me. I wasn't there; I couldn't relate to how severe the emotional trauma could be. Ours was a generation in upheaval—a perfect storm of forces demanding change.

As this reality seriously affected other people, I went from one form of stimulation to another—from pride in my image and the flattery of acceptance at the entrance of the business world to the concentrated rush and exaltation of experiencing pleasure in my abilities as a skydiver. I also switched from numbing my senses with alcohol to coloring my senses with marijuana.

My life's priorities were skydiving first, then my relationship with Julie. She had school and I was okay with that. My third priority was hanging out with old friends, doing unproductive and unhealthy activities. As my quest in sport parachuting dominated my thoughts and emotions, these other priorities had to be squeezed into my commitment to the sport, which had become my burning passion.

There seems to be something commendable about doing something with 100 percent of everything that you are and enthusiastically incorporating all of your abilities. The glamour and glory of shiny airplanes, the dashing role of being a skydiver with helmet, goggles, new boots, and the latest gadgets, made me feel like some kind of superhero. I let the light of my endeavors shine on and cover up the negatives that were popping up in my life.

During this time my mom and dad's twenty-three-year marriage officially ended. Dad's alcoholism, which bred progressive brokenness, their ongoing arguments, and financial ruin had made their marriage terminal. Shortly after my father left our beautiful home in a peaceful neighborhood, my mom was forced to sell the house. She used the small amount she got out of the sale to make a tiny down payment on a humble home in a quiet community about ten miles from our familiar surroundings. It was now just my mom, me, and my brother, Robert, who was fourteen years old.

I did not fully understand how disastrous this was for our family. My sisters, Barbara and Marilyn, were both married and had newborns. Consequently, my mom pretty much had to venture out on her own after having been a full-time wife and mother for almost twenty-four years.

Robert and I and a few friends hastily unloaded our house and all of our belongings, packed them onto a moving truck, and whisked away to our new location in Parma Heights, Ohio. To me it was just another day in my life. How insensitive to mom and my brother I must've been—like picking up the shattered vase of our family's history, loading the pieces into a brown grocery bag, and thinking, *We can just glue it all together.*

Soon after, Dan got the biggest contract our skydiving team had ever landed. It was a large church carnival with about fifteen thousand people in attendance. Almost all of them would be witnessing something like this for the first time, and we were obligated to give them their money's worth. Dan and I and two other gifted skydivers—a four-man team—had this assignment. We carefully discussed our exit patterns and the choreography we were to perform in free fall as we were climbing to jump altitude. Our landing area would be a tiny patch of green grass densely surrounding a large church, with new houses in every direction. There was absolutely no margin for error.

Before we got to our desired altitude of ten thousand feet, the pilot received a sharp command from the control tower at Cleveland Hopkins Airport. Our pilot, Walt, had properly filed a flight plan for this show jump, but as the controller was tracking our plane's ascent, the officer said, "Do not go above three thousand feet. You are in controlled airspace. There will be large aircraft on final approach." Obviously our pilot was under authority to comply. But as we got over the church property, Dan looked at me and said, "They paid for skydiving. We're gonna show them free fall."

After we exited the plane, the first ten seconds of free fall covered about a thousand feet. So as we were forming a four-man star, we were already at fifteen hundred feet. We should have been under open parachutes at two thousand feet!

I could see that Dan was going to keep going. I started to track toward the target and popped my chute about three seconds later. Going low was dangerously stupid and very scary. I faced directly into the target and pulled my legs up to cut wind resistance. I glided swiftly over the front of the large crowd and heard the announcer saying over a loudspeaker, "Here comes Mickey Robinson. Girls, he's nineteen years old. Keep your eyes on him."

I executed a radical 180-degree turn barely above their heads, landing on both feet and standing up about thirty feet in front of them. My beautiful red, white, and blue parachute fell gently on top of the crowd. It was simply spectacular. It could've played well in any movie theater. The audience rushed to see me the way groupies rushed the stage at rock concerts. Dan and the rest of the team had landed about a thousand feet away, so it turned out to be kind of an unplanned solo act.

I found that more than satisfying, and it gave me an epiphany—the realization of a level of performance and skill I'd never even seen before, and it flowed out of me naturally, like the water over the majesty of Niagara Falls.

Afterward, while Dan and the rest of the team put the parachutes in the trunks of our cars, Julie and I walked around snacking on festival food. I shook hands with hundreds of appreciative onlookers. As a beautiful fire-in-the-sky sunset yielded to the dusk, I was about to start my car when Julie leaned over, kissed me, then looked into my eyes and said, "I'm so proud of you."

I smiled and looked away, yet somehow I felt that there was a slight disconnect between us. I didn't know if it was me or her or something else. It surely couldn't have anything to do with skydiving, because that was 100 percent pure pleasure. I had entertained all these people, and at the same time, completely satisfied myself.

King Solomon once wrote, "The eyes of man are never satisfied."[2] I wouldn't have believed this truth if he had appeared right in front of me with a crown on his head! I was consumed. What had been my childhood fantasy had become real. Experience is a more powerful teacher than learned information.

As ecstatic as these experiences had become, it produced a thirst for more. So King Solomon *was* right, but I couldn't see that because the brightness of the moment blinded me from the deeper truth.

Early evening the next day, I went to visit a close friend of Julie's and mine. Linda and her high-school steady boyfriend, Grant, had double-dated with us more times than I could count. She'd had minor foot surgery and had casts on both feet at the same time. She was in Southwest Community Hospital in Berea,

Ohio, a suburb just south of Cleveland. Julie was still at work and Grant was working an extra shift. So I went to visit Linda alone.

When I walked into the hospital room, I found her in a wheelchair. She looked great, as always. Our conversation was totally upbeat. We joked around with our usual fond bantering about each other's partners. I had a high degree of respect for Linda and her intelligence.

When it was time to go, I gave her a friendly kiss on the cheek and said, "See you later this week."

As I headed down the hallway, I heard, "Young man, you're a very good-looking boy. You have such nice skin!" I turned and saw the elderly man who'd paid me this kind compliment in a heavy accent. It was summer and I had my usual bronze tan. I felt a little embarrassed, but I thanked him as I headed for the exit.

Walking down the hall and out to the car, I was aware of how gloomy and confining that place seemed. I told myself, *I could never stand one night in here.*

After work the next day, I raced out to our drop zone in Brunswick, where we were going to try out the pilot's new airplane. Four of us were scheduled to make this jump. After takeoff and before we could reach our maximum altitude of 12,500 feet, the pilot started having engine trouble. Somewhere around five thousand feet, the motor sputtered. So Walt asked us to jump out early, giving him an empty plane to deal with the problem. We landed normally and waited for him to tell us the scoop. He assured us it was some kind of minor problem with the carburetor adjustment. No big deal. We packed our parachutes and headed home early, a little disappointed because we were always eager to jump.

The night was young, so I phoned my friend Roger. He informed me that everyone was going to Danny's apartment to get stoned. I dropped my brother off at home; Robert wasn't a part of this scene and I hadn't told him about the secret society of potheads.

When I arrived at Danny's apartment, the pot party had already begun. With psychedelic lights pulsating and music playing, they were using a newly acquired smoking instrument called a hookah. They were also using marijuana that some of the Vietnam War veterans had smuggled back home from the war zone. That combination took getting high to a new level of intensity. This stuff was like mega-marijuana in potency. The room quickly became cloudy as each of us took a turn drawing on the pipe, making it glow red.

I sensed "bad vibes" that evening, which were not just an effect of the drug. There was something else in the atmosphere besides music and smoke. Everyone was taking turns making snide put-down remarks about me being a skydiver. I didn't care to defend something that was so valuable to me. So I decided to call it a night.

As I started to leave, Pete, one of Vietnam vets who had just returned from the war, said he wanted to catch a ride home with me. As he got into my car, he looked in the backseat and saw my parachute and gear neatly stacked in the corner. "Is this what you use when you crash?" The word *crash* was drug lingo for what happens when a stoned person falls asleep wherever they're hanging out. His sarcastic attempt to be witty was eerily strange and creepy to me. He laughed, but it did not seem funny at all to me.

My friends didn't understand that for me getting "high" was about altitude, not drugs. I'd gotten to the point where hassles, conflicts, and issues could all be left behind as I stepped off my newly discovered place of detached pleasure—a separated state of being called *free fall*. In my mind, as Frank Sinatra put it, "I did it my way."

Little did I know that life as I knew it would soon change drastically and never be the same again. Ever.

Eleven

Mortal Contact

On August 15, 1968, the ambulance sped down the streets, carrying my badly burned body. Deep in my memory reverberated a prayer called the act of contrition: *Oh my God, I am heartily sorry for having offended thee.*

When we jolted to a stop, the doors exploded open and paramedics urgently slid me out from the back of the vehicle.

I detest all my sins because of Thy just punishment, but most of all because they offend Thee.

As they wheeled me from the silent darkness into the blinding red light, signage above declared *Emergency.* The trauma team frantically went to work on me. As pieces of my jumpsuit were cut away, I heard a voice say, "Lots of third-degree burns covering most of the right side of his body. Very severe on the left leg as well, and probable head trauma."

Something sharp slid into my left hand as soaking wet towels covered my arms and legs. I watched a vast network of tubes crisscross above me as a nurse peeled the melted sock from my right foot.

Oh Lord, who art all good and worthy of all my love...

"This guy is a mess. Has somebody called his family?"

I firmly resolve, with the help of Thy grace, to sin no more and to avoid the near occasion of sin.

"We called the family. Better call a priest."

101

Yeah, like right now.

When they were finally able to reach my mother, she was told, "Your son, Mickey, has been injured in a plane crash. Please come immediately to the admissions desk at Southwest General in Berea."

My girlfriend was working that evening at her summer job when she picked up the phone and heard my mother's frantic voice. "Mickey's plane crashed. We've got to go to the hospital right away. He's hurt real bad."

"What? Is he...?"

"No. He's gonna be okay."

They wouldn't let Julie in, but my mother was allowed to see me for sixty seconds. Although heavily dosed with morphine, I whispered, "Don't blame skydiving, Mom." Like a zealot singing hymns while being burned at the stake, I was ready to defend sport parachuting as not guilty.

After this brief and urgent encounter, I was taken from the ER to the surgical floor. Rapid preparation was administered under a cloud of deadly worst-case medical scenario.

From somewhere deep inside gushed a passionate request. I insisted that my mother find Father John. I didn't want to go under anesthesia until I received last rites from a priest. By some miracle, my mother located the man who'd terrorized my Catholic boyhood. Although he'd long since been moved to another church from St. Michael's, Father John drove to the hospital that night to anoint me for burial.

This time he didn't scare me. His once-booming voice sounded soft and far away as he began the rite of extreme unction: *"Per istam sanctam unctionem..."* (Through this holy anointing...).

The ancient prayer called me back from behind the heavy curtain of shock. I didn't know what the Latin words meant, but they penetrated to a place far beyond hearing.

"Et suam piissimam misericordiam indulgeat tibi Dominus quidquid deliquisti." (May the Lord forgive you whatever sins you have committed.)

Father John dipped his huge thumb into the tiny vial of holy oil and lightly touched the charred remains of my eyes, nose, lips, ears, and hands. I remembered my catechism. Whatever sins I'd committed through these five senses had now been covered by the forgiving hand of God. Strangely, the locations on my body that the sacrament is designated to be anointed with oil were the five most severely damaged places on my body.

Father John had barely finished his prayer when an orderly wheeled me down an echoing hallway into a room filled with nightmarish pain. The nurses pulled a curtain around me so I couldn't see the other patients, but I knew they were there. I could hear groaning all around me.

This was the Intensive Care Unit, a place where human beings lay in the twilight between life and death. ICU is a surrealistic realm where committed, passionate caregivers focus all their attention on keeping the flame of life burning on people who are hanging on to nearly nothing.

Although this hospital was hardly prepared for a disaster like me, the staff tried their best to determine my condition and decide what to do about it. After the immediate examination triage, the chief surgeon determined that I probably wouldn't make it through the night—I would most likely die of shock before morning. Still, the staff fluttered nonstop to rotate IV bottles, blood transfusions, 100 percent pure oxygen, and just enough pain medication to keep me from slipping over the edge.

Almost half of my nineteen-year-old body was now a black, oozing wound. Even though I was barely conscious, a phrase that was previously never part of my vocabulary echoed over and over in my mind: *God, I'm sorry. I want to live! Please give me another chance.*

The pain was excruciating. I lay helplessly on my back, unable to move, my entire body throbbing as masked faces and hands darted in and out of my scope of vision. I slipped away from consciousness.

About twelve hours after my admission, morning dawned. And I was still alive.

According to the doctors, I was so near death they waived many restrictions, allowing special friends and family to visit me. From their standpoint it would be the last chance these loved ones would have to see me and say good-bye. Still, they excluded my father, deciding that seeing him might upset me because of the personal trauma of our relationship. How horrible that must've been for him. However, I was oblivious to all this.

None of my visitors was prepared for what they saw upon entering ICU that morning. In addition to the horrendous burns, my head had swollen way beyond its normal size. The right side of my face was charred and blackened flesh. A gaping laceration from the right corner of my mouth and up past what used to be my right ear exposed the inside of my jaw. The upper and lower eyelids of my right eye were burned and retracted. Some people actually fainted after taking one look at me.

I was blind in my right eye and unable to move as a stream of visitors leaned over the safety bars to see me. I only remember a few of them.

Jim asked, "What happened?" Obviously he knew what happened. His question came out of ghastly shock from seeing me in such horrible condition. Jim had lived one house away growing up. We met each other when were only three years old.

"Planes don't fly too good on the ground," I told my lifelong friend whose face registered complete horror.

When Grant came to visit later that day, I stared blankly at him and said, "What're you doing here? Why aren't you at work?"

"What do you mean?" His voice trembled as he almost broke down into tears.

I didn't know how badly I was hurt, but I could sense their devastated emotions.

When my brother, Robert, came to visit me, he had a swab of smelling salts taped on his left forearm, in case he needed it to keep from passing out.

My life was a blur. Every fifteen minutes or so, nurses made adjustments to the life-support systems. I experienced lapses of consciousness.

Night after night, the doctors expected me to die before morning. Still, they engaged in a heroic effort to keep me alive and battle the possible complications. Every two hours, the nurses had to wrap my burned legs, torso, and arms in clean towels and soak them with silver nitrate to try to protect these severely damaged areas. The dead tissue was a fertile breeding ground for all types of infections.

My right hand was so severely damaged there was little probability of it being at all functional. The skin was burned through all the layers, and the intense heat caused the tendons to constrict tightly, pulling my hand closed. My little finger and ring finger were fused together, and even though the doctors went to extreme preventive measures, it became so infected the chief surgeon planned to amputate my forearm and hand.

The most dreaded burn treatment was called *debridement*. Without anesthetic, the surgeon had to cut, snip, and scrape the dead tissue with scalpels and scissors, to the level where there was live tissue and blood flow. This had to be done in any area I was about to receive skin grafting for.

"Hello, Mr. Robinson. How're you feeling? We're here to do a little cleanup on you today." The nurse and the surgeon arrived and set up a sterile field around my head, neck, and upper body.

Then they cut away all the tissue around my eye socket, my right cheek, and the entire right side of my head. I saw the doctor pulling with a clamp instrument, and I heard a crunching sound as all but a small portion of the cartilage in my right ear was cut into pieces and thrown away. *Painful* is not an accurate enough word to describe this experience. But I stoically remained silent, thinking I was supposed to take it like a man.

However, I didn't feel like a man anymore. Everything I thought made me a normal human being had vanished in the crash impact and flames.

I had lost all my physical gifts—charismatic glib talk, physical talents, relational confidence...my self-image. I had been stripped down to the lowest level of human existence: consciousness, shattered emotions, extreme pain, and a rapidly declining prognosis.

My injuries were catastrophically critical and unstable. The worst thing about burns and the other wounds are the complications that could easily follow. In just a few weeks, my finely tuned athletic physique of 175 pounds withered to 98 pounds. Infection was rampant over many areas of my skin. I had a contusion of my brain from the impact of my head going a deadly speed upon hitting the tree. More times than not I was in deep unconsciousness—a combination of head trauma, general anesthetics from surgery, and the strongest pain medication allowed. Unfortunately, no medication could touch this kind of pain.

My legs and muscles were totally weak. They also became straight and rigid. The anterior nervous system from my knees downward was withered, and both legs from the knees down, including my feet, were unresponsive.

Infections got into my circulatory system, and microorganisms started living in my bloodstream. I was bleeding ten pints a day. I completely emptied the blood bank at Southwest Hospital. On one occasion seventy-five people left a party to come and donate blood for me.

My nervous system was so sensitive and traumatized that when I was awake, if someone even bumped the bed, it felt like my whole body was jolted with a sledgehammer.

In spite of the passionate and constant medical attention being applied to me, each complication made my condition worse, and they were compounding upon one another. As the nursery rhyme goes, "All the king's horses and all the king's men were desperately trying to put Mickey back together again."

In the midst of this deadly downward spiral, medically unexplainable things took place. Skin grafts that should never have worked were 100 percent successful. As the doctor removed the bandage from a large area at the back of my neck after the skin graft, and he saw that all the tissue was fresh and healthy, he gasped, "Oh my God!"

Dan Harding came to see me every day. Even when I was in a deep state of unconsciousness, whenever he stepped off the elevator a hundred feet or so away, I instantly sprang wide awake, completely alert.

On one occasion, Dan came to visit a few minutes after I saw how destroyed my right hand was for the first time. "My hand looks like a piece of crap," I said harshly.

He looked at me sternly and said, "Don't you ever say anything like that again. You are going to get better and get out of here. You'll be just fine." Dan would never let me think or say anything negative.

Another skydiving buddy, Jerry, drove well over an hour to see me, even though we had known each other only a short time. At first, he could only sit outside the ICU unit. But he came anyway, wanting to be close to me even though he couldn't actually see me. He finally got put on the list of authorized visitors.

One time when he came to see me, I was so weak I didn't have enough strength to speak. He sat there, clutched my left hand,

and steadily, rhythmically squeezed it. As he did this, I felt waves of life energy being pumped into me. Toward the end of Jerry's visit, I was strong enough to have a clear and meaningful conversation with him.

These visits taught me that being touched with compassion and words of life can have an immeasurable power over natural law. Light is a superior force over darkness.

Several times I had spiritual experiences that I had no prior knowledge of or previous interest in.

My sister's father-in-law was a prominent surgeon who had just returned from thirteen months of volunteer surgical work on Vietnamese civilians. He had seen the worst possible injuries, including burns that had assaulted human bodies by way of modern instruments of warfare. In spite of our age difference, this doctor and I had enjoyed a close friendship. We had several common interests that sparked lively discussions. He was a private airplane pilot and an avid investor in the stock market. And we shared some of the same ideas about worldviews and political scenarios. He was also well aware that physically, I was a professional athlete.

His first visit was in the early days right after my accident. He examined me and went over my case with the chief surgeon. After that medical confab, Dr. Bill told me, "Mickey, I want you to eat everything they put in front of you." As he walked out of the room and down the corridor to the exit, I moved right alongside him. As he approached the door, I was perplexed as to why he wasn't even looking at me. When his foot stepped on the automatic door opener, the door swung open toward us, and it went right through me as if I was made out of nothing! Instantly I was snapped back into my body as if attached to an invisible bungee cord.

Another time, I visited the place I worked, gliding past various departments where I saw and recognized people.

About ten days after my crash, I found myself standing in

the middle of a social gathering that was outdoors. I knew all the people attending fairly well. They were having a picnic-style celebration, but everyone was sober and sad. It was supposed to be a happy event, but they were all upset because of me.

I'd never heard of people having experiences outside of the physical body. I now believe that I was teetering so close to death that my spirit traveled to places I was familiar with or toward people I had a meaningful relationship with. These experiences were spontaneous and had nothing to do with me initiating them.

These phenomena should have been thought-provoking. But I wasn't able to analyze what was going on with me. I was consumed with the immediate, which was extreme desperation. My view of the outside world from my hospital bed in ICU was limited to looking straight up at the ceiling or at visitors who would lean over the safety bars. Most of my interaction involved surgery, daily bandage changing, and maintenance of a number of life support systems.

The ICU floor did not contain individual rooms but sections with curtains pulled around them. Consequently, I was aware of most of the other patients who were being cared for. One man who had worked in an economy gas station had been robbed of thirty dollars. The thief commanded him to walk away, then shot him in the back with a shotgun. He was paralyzed from the waist down. Over and over, he asked, "Can I have more Life Savers?" Apparently the candy was some kind of comfort in his suffering.

The man directly across from me was in a full body cast from a car accident. I sensed he was an older man, but somehow I felt he was going to make it.

One man was a victim of a practical joke at work. Someone had slipped an oxygen hose into the back pocket of his apron while he worked on his machine. When a spark ignited, the whole lower portion of his body was completely burned. His wife was attentive and loving with him, cleansing him and cutting his hair. She told her story to my family as they told my story to her. When he got out, I was happy for him. But I stayed, and no one was talking about me getting out.

In the middle of the night I heard the greatest human agony. The moaning, the repeated requests for pain medicine, hysterical cries of "Get me out of here!" When I was conscious in those dark, gloomy hours of the night, I expressed my own agony and misery.

My mom often asked the doctors, "Is he out of the woods yet?"

They started out saying, "He's very, very critical." Later they simply said, "He probably won't make it." But my mom never accepted that I could die. She was the only one who believed I would survive.

Medically the doctors were running out of options. My chief surgeon even came in after hours and brought me a twelve-pack of beer! I needed to be hydrated, and it didn't matter what the liquid was. I tried to drink some, but it didn't taste appealing to me.

I didn't eat much either. After taking a few bites, food just spewed out of my mouth.

Out of therapeutic ideas, my doctor called in a highly respected burn specialist from a major school of medicine in our area. After a thorough examination, the specialist described my condition in highly technical medical terms. But his concluding statement was easy to understand: "There is simply nothing I have to offer this young man."

From that point on, the ministers of medicine gave up trying to save my life. They just waited for death to take me.

No one could blame these physicians for their opinions. Scientifically and medically, all was hopeless. I was entering the darkest place in "the valley of the shadow of death." But there was one element missing from the diagnosis summary: the power of a supernatural God.

Twelve

The Last Day

There are two common denominators that unite all human beings and span time, social stature, education, and all forms of beliefs: Everyone is born, and everyone will die.

Philosophers, religious minds, psychologists, and scientists all have had to deal with death—the inevitable reality of all humanity. For all their grand efforts of opinions, theories, and oftentimes far-out speculations, only two possibilities remain: there is an afterlife, or there is oblivion—a never-ending state of nothingness. The most common conclusion drawn from the latter is that there is no God.

Four or five weeks before this juncture in my life, I was oblivious to thoughts about death, an afterlife, right or wrong, and the existence of a personal God. I was strong at what I was doing, accelerating in my abilities, and blinded by the light of my own image. I had my act together. I was invincible, unstoppable. Until I collided into human mortality. Now I was barely living from one breath to the next.

Having multiple infections both inside and on the outside of my body, and practically zero nutrition, massive blood loss and lack of sufficient body fluids resulted in an out-of-control fever. Because of the burns and external wounds, ice packs and alcohol rubs could not be applied. Instead, a vinyl sheet was placed under me, with plastic tubes networking through it that circulated a refrigerated fluid to try to reduce the temperature. I was freezing on the outside from the cold underneath me, but I was burning up on the inside from fever, shivering and shaking so violently that the metal bars on both sides of my bed were clanging.

An eerie feeling crept over me that felt like switches inside my body were being turned to the off position. My organs were shutting down and my breathing was rapid and very shallow, like a weak panting. Out of mercy, the doctors maxed out my pain medicine.

I was completely unconscious, unable to hear or see or move, when I experienced another spiritual phenomenon.

The chief surgeon was standing on the right side of my bed, holding my chart. He was speaking to a nurse on the left side of my bed. I heard him say, "When Mr. Robinson dies, I want you to completely sanitize this entire area. Then I want you to move Mr. Clark's bed into this spot."

No, no, I thought. *That's wrong. That is not going to happen.*

To this day I remember the tone of his voice, the look of resolve on their faces, and my resistance to what they were saying was soon to happen. But I had zero ability to respond. (Lesson to remember: be careful what you say around people you think aren't there!)

Later that night, during the eleven o'clock shift change, a family friend who was a police officer snuck into the hospital through the service elevator. Bob Giuliani used to come over to our house and have coffee on a regular basis. He knew I was in bad shape, so he ignored the rules and got in to see me. He had a tiny police flashlight with him, and just twelve inches from my face, he said, "Mickey, how are you doing?"

"I don't know." Though I didn't elaborate, he could tell what I meant.

"Italians died hard," he said—just before a nurse found him and kicked him out.

Though I received my eleven o'clock pain shot, which put me out for a bit, most of the night I was burning with fever and shaking violently.

After the 7 AM shift change, the chief surgeon came in to examine me. Then he went back to his office and called my sister Barbara. She had just given birth to my nephew a few weeks before, so she couldn't be a part of the long-term vigil that most the family was making.

He told her, "Barbara, you'd better get here right now. I just saw your brother and he will be not here this afternoon when I make my rounds."

That morning the nurse tilted my head up a little bit to help me breathe a little easier. I then experienced another unearthly ability. Looking above the bed, I saw right through the wall into a room with bright overhead lights and stainless-steel tables surrounded by instruments on counters.

While this was going on, my brother showed up. Robert stood at the left side of my bed, wearing my best golf shirt. "Robbie, how did you get in here?" I asked matter-of-factly.

"What do you mean?"

"This is the morgue," I said emphatically.

A look of concern clouded his face. "You're okay, Mick. Don't worry about that."

I'm sure he thought I was delirious and hallucinating, but I wasn't. I was actually seeing through the wall into that very room. The vision vanished as I talked to Robert about it. After a few minutes, my brother left the room to sit outside in the tense waiting area.

My fever and shaking ramped up again, and the pain medicine was not at all effective.

Then suddenly, like a butterfly breaking out of a cocoon, my inner being, my spirit, and my soul separated from my physical body. I felt my lower torso and legs go through the mattress and bed frame. Then my spiritual being was poised perpendicular to my broken body. Immediately I was transported into another dimension: a spiritual world!

I looked myself over. My spiritual body was whole. My right hand was not mangled but perfect. No burns, no scars, no blemishes at all.

Multiple things were simultaneously revealed to me. Amazingly, I knew I was a spirit, I had a soul, and I lived in a physical body in the natural world. But I was no longer in the natural world, the created physical universe. This spiritual place was not earthly, and everything operated differently in the spiritual realm.

The colors were far more than just more colorful. They radiated with depth and brilliance. I saw the shapes of things I was passing with razor-sharp clarity and high definition. I observed their full dimensions, as if I had 360-degree sight while looking straight ahead. Emotions were far more intense; I was in a state of shock, amazement, and awe.

This spirit man was the real me, and this spiritual heavenly place was more real than anything I'd ever experienced in the physical world through my five senses and with my intellectual mind. My whole conscious perception was in a different mode of operation. Before I could even try to conceive a question, the truth resonated within me. Everything was brilliant and engaging.

What's happening to me? What about the airplane crash? Where's my body and what happened to it? Rational thinking, logic and reason, and natural laws were obliterated by the newness of spiritual consciousness.

As shocking and amazing as all this was, there was one aspect that was predominant and constant. I was captivated by the reality of knowing and understanding eternity. Everything in the created universe and the physical plane is related to chronological time. Something new will eventually get old. Everything that begins will have an end. Living things—animal or plant—have a beginning of life that will end in physical death. The entire physical universe is contained in time. All of our thoughts, feelings, and emotions, our pain and pleasure, are all just a blip on the screen of eternity. The natural mind cannot comprehend this; it takes spiritual enlightenment and a spiritual mind to understand how spiritual things operate.

Enraptured in the wonder of it all, I was drawn by an invisible force toward an opening—a portal of pure white light. As I gazed at this dazzling light, a compelling feeling deep inside made me yearn to enter into it. It was brighter than a thousand suns but peacefully comforting. Slightly elevated above my glide path, the light was the center of my focus in what I was experiencing. Traveling toward it I understood that this portal was a gateway. As I got closer, I could feel the peace that was the nature of this passage.

As I neared the light, I felt something like a pressure against my right side. I turned to my right in response to this feeling and saw…blackness.

It was blacker than the blackest black, an abyss of complete emptiness, and I knew it was forever. It would be like someone picked you up and dipped you into a swimming pool of black ink. However, you would be super conscious, but with no sight, no feeling of touch, void of all life, with the unending hopeless remorse that this state would go on forever.

The condition of a soul enclosed in this bottomless darkness is beyond dreadful. You would have passions and burning desires for everything, but you would know only total separation from the source of all life. Dreams of being somebody or desires wanting to be fulfilled would be forever overcome, replaced by ongoing conscious nightmares of dark despair. This aloneness would be final. Nonnegotiable. Never-ending. Forever.

As I gazed at this darkness, unimaginable terror intensified. I actually felt what this separation would be like. Infinite solitary confinement. This edge of darkness began to eclipse the pure white portal of light I was about to enter. Then, like a drowning man gasping for air, my spirit screamed out the same words I desperately prayed when the paramedics brought me from the crash site and many times in ICU: "Please God, I want to live. I want to be alive. Please give me another chance!"

Thirteen

Caught Up

As those desperate words gushed from my spirit being, I slipped through the remaining sliver of pure white light. I was drawn out of the darkness and thrust through this radiant portal, bursting into the very presence of almighty God.

Instantly I knew I would never die and would live forever and ever. I was having the same kind of simultaneous spiritual comprehension that occurred when my spirit man entered that mystical heavenly place, but this time I was comprehending the nature of God and the glory of His majesty. I could feel His presence somewhere to my immediate left as I stood straight up with my arms stretched high, being bathed in the pure, undiluted, perfect love of God.

This living, breathing glory engulfed all of everything and me. This glory was not just a feeling or emotional experience. It was a Presence. Standing in this pure radiance, I did not see any image, form, or shape, yet I knew it was a Person. The regal majesty of this Person pierced me like countless laser beams.

God is infinite in every direction. From His throne emanates all power, all wisdom, all ecstatic splendor, and unquestionable authority, all governed by unrelenting supreme love.

I knew this was the real heaven. King David wrote, "In your presence there is fullness of joy; at your right hand are pleasures forevermore."[3] His inspired writings three thousand years ago were now happening to me in the immediate manifested presence of God Himself.

Although I did not see His personal image, a heavenly throne, or any other living beings, I knew I was in the center and at the source and sustaining power of all life. What I was seeing and experiencing was more magnificent than the human language can describe. I believe I was standing in what the Bible describes the "pure river of water of life" flowing from God's throne.[4] It was passing through me somewhere between my hips and my knees.

I felt as if I was seeing radiation with my naked eye, a rapidly vibrating glory stream that had particles of gold within it. This living water caused me to be in perfect harmony with the Spirit of God, at one with Him. I was more alive than any condition of being alive on earth. I was infused with perfect love and perfect peace.

Everything this river touched burst into new life—new creation life. I was enraptured by an immense awareness, an overwhelming knowing that all human beings are made to be connected and tuned to His holy vibration. The spectacular, radiant energy and majesty that was emanating everywhere in every direction did not outshine the preeminence of being in the presence of the Person.

The colors I saw are unlike earthly colors. Everything had the appearance of translucent jewels with flowing colors, but I could see right through them. The nature of heaven was so different because it was made out of different kinds of materials than the physical world, and this "stuff" operated in very different ways.

There were no shadows in heaven. Light came into everything, and it also radiated out of everything. There was an overwhelming, all-pervasive awareness of the magnitude of my being in the center of a great expanse that extended everywhere. Indescribable shapes and colors all vibrated like an orchestra of visual harmony.

Everything was living, nothing was just material, and everything glorified God!

In this heavenly place there was nothing that was not completely pure and clean. I was not only set free, I was also innocent—and accepted by the only one who really mattered. Accepted as a son by the Father who would care for me forever.

Being in the actual presence of God created explosive dynamics and everlasting values within me. Unquestionably, I knew this really was God. Out of the confines of my physical body and the clatter of life on earth, I was receiving an unfiltered experience with the purest power, Spirit to spirit. I realized that knowing God from my understanding of what the Scriptures teach was not about philosophical ponderings or rational understanding, but rather about intimacy. To be intimate with God meant knowing Him and being one with Him.

I knew the magnitude of all the awesome things I was seeing and experiencing would continue to transform me for the rest of my life.

The one thing that caused the greatest awe in this experience, which affected me more than anything else, was knowing, feeling, and hearing from God Himself the unrelenting, personal, everlasting love He has for me.

How did this happen? Extreme grace and mercy from the true and living God was released when I uttered a weak but desperately authentic plea toward God—"I'm sorry! Please give me another chance!"—inspired by a subconscious remembrance of a priest who made me memorize a prayer. My by-the-skin-of-my-teeth cries for help to a God I had paid no attention to were similar to the thief who cried out while dying on a cross beside Jesus. I had been given a gift that no one could ever earn.

What I was receiving was beyond conventional understanding. What I needed could not be obtained through some systematic knowledge, from being good enough, by learning mystical gifts, or through some form of excelling in human potential. What I needed was exactly what I had run out of: life. Now I was receiving new life from the very Source of all life.

Seeing the beauty of a little child or hearing of a kind act demonstrated in the midst of a cruel, unjust situation causes us to perceive the innocence of a person. But this is only relative to our definition or comparative experience of innocence. The innocence of heaven, however, is a state of being, as if you never did, heard, or saw anything that wasn't anything but pure and perfect. It exists only in the Pure One and can only be given by Him.

God existed in absolute purity before creation. Through our sins, every one of us is guilty before a holy God. But God, who is rich in mercy, because of His great love with which He loves us, even in our state of spiritual deadness, can make us alive together with Him through the Anointed One.

According to the law, the Lamb of God had to be innocent and perfect in order to be a worthy sacrifice. No human being could pull that off. So God sent His Son, to be born innocent and pure. Thirty-three years later, Jesus stood before Pilate on the day the priests were examining the lambs for slaughter for the Passover. Mocked, falsely accused, and beaten, He stood before Pontius Pilate, who said, "I find no fault in this Man."[5] The Roman governor's examination was accurate: this Lamb was faultless. One eternally innocent Man canceled the debt of all humankind. Now, that is absolute freedom!

In heaven there exists nothing but purity. No remembrance of any wrongdoing, no regrets that someone you knew is not there with you. Absolute fullness and completeness, with nothing missing or broken. There is no memory or consciousness of anything negative. All types of fear are completely gone. Shame, guilt, remorse, all wiped out. Trauma—whether physical, emotional, or spiritual—is erased as if it never happened. Even muscle memory that was caused by experiences of flight and fright, natural responses designed for self-protection, are cast into the sea of forgetfulness.

Illicit pleasures of addictions, inappropriate relationships, and selfish ambition—all that is tolerated as normal on earth—cannot come near the holiness of the Lord. Any form of sorrow, from the slightest disappointment to the incurable pain of tragedy and loss in human suffering, is cleansed away, without any of our own effort to process.

This is why we can understand "God will wipe away every tear" (Revelation 21:4). Every moment of pain associated with every single tear is gone! And He turns our grieving into dancing—joyful celebration of thanksgiving.

I was shocked when my spirit left my body and entered into that mystical realm, where I was stunned by eternity and saw that hopeless abyss of darkness. It was infinitely more shocking and astounding to be in the third heaven, in the holy presence of God. All things had become new. I would always belong there, and I knew that I would never be alone. There was a constant and overwhelming awareness that the Lord Himself would take care of me forever.

Fourteen

Transcending Worlds

Although I had never heard of anyone having these kinds of spiritual experiences, I had seen various religious artwork depicting heaven—the Lord Himself standing on a cloud with winged angels playing harps around Him. I think most people try to perceive God from what they've seen and heard, framing their concepts and imagery through the lens of human understanding. The supernatural realm is so unworldly, so unnatural, that human words are insufficient to describe what it is really like.

The Bible states, "In the beginning God created the heavens and the earth."[6] Heavens is plural. I believe the first heaven is the earth's atmosphere, all of the various stratospheres, and all that can be seen with the naked eye and through telescopes. The first heaven is the natural realm above the earth.

When I left my body in the hospital, I believe I entered a spiritual realm the Bible implies is the second heaven. While in the second heaven, I saw and understood things I couldn't have on earth. This is the place the apostle Paul referred to in his letter to believers in Ephesus when he spoke of the wisdom of God being "known by the church to the principalities and powers in the heavenly *places.*"[7] When people of varying spiritual beliefs see angels, demons, or other spiritual powers and entities, I believe they are seeing into this realm. I believe astral projection operates in this realm. Some people who have out-of-body experiences or go into another spiritual dimension enter the second heaven, but I do not believe this realm is the heaven of God.

I entered what I believe is the third heaven when I slipped through the portal of white light and burst into the presence of God. The apostle Paul wrote that he knew a man who was caught up to the third heaven and then into Paradise, indicating a place of blissful, ecstatic relationship with God.[8] Paul refrained from speaking about his experiences partly because he did not want to appear to be boasting about himself for being spiritual.

This mystery that he stated was hidden for ages concerned the unsearchable riches of our Lord Jesus Christ, which was now available to everyone, even to outsiders—those who were not the people of God. I was certainly an outsider.

It was years before I was able to speak to anybody about these experiences. To this day I do my best not to brag about things that I had nothing to do with concerning my miraculous and continual transformation. But in this I will brag: I know the love of God for me personally, and the power of His love continually blows me away.

One word that might be descriptive of everything I experienced is *transcendent*. Everything about heaven goes above and beyond what you know, can think of, or would try to imagine. Many people have asked me, "How long did it last?" I can't answer that because the experience transcended time, space, and all things that we know about the natural world.

Another word that might be helpful to illustrate my heavenly encounter is *belonging*. My passport was changed and I became a citizen of heaven. It's astounding that something so strange and unfamiliar could have the surprising comfort of feeling at home in the celestial location called heaven.

Power is another word that illustrates my heavenly encounter. Two of the Greek words that define God's power are helpful in understanding my experience. One of the Greek words is *exousia*, God's absolute legal and sovereign authority. Another word for power is *dunimas*, meaning miraculous, active power with the ability to do anything. Not merely power capable of action, but power in action.

How did I not cower in the face of divine authority? And how could I not be crushed by the intensity of unlimited power? I not only had the right to stand in His authority and *dunimas* power, I was absorbing them into my very being. How can this possibly be? Grace. Very amazing grace. I was being empowered by the strongest form of energy, and I was also being soothed with the most comforting form of rest.

While standing in the River of Life in the third heaven, a vision opened before me. Unlike today's flat-screen TVs, the vision was like a hologram with depth and dimension—supernatural 3-D. Progressively I began to see things that would span the next approximately six and one-half years of my life, supernaturally presented in sequence, like a spiritual version of virtual reality. I observed many things that I didn't understand, yet some of them caused me to have strong feelings about their significance. In the vision, I saw people I didn't know, yet I had some kind of important relationship with them and the activities going on around them. Also, some of the people who were already in my life were specifically involved in some of what I was seeing and feeling.

The first thing I saw was the Brunswick Flying Ranch—the place where our skydiving team based our operation. I was looking down from what I perceived to be about seventy-five feet above the field. I could see the three of us who were professionals loading into the airplane along with the two students we were training. I then observed the trailer that was our office building and noticed nonhuman beings hiding along the sides of the building and behind objects like parked cars. I had the perception that they were invisible to the people on the ground. No one walking around could see them, but they were very real and there was some kind of "spirit war" going on.

The scene changed and I was in a room where I saw musicians rehearsing with electric guitars, drums, and large amplifiers. Then, like an acceleration of fast-forwarding picture frames, I saw a panoramic view of huge rock-music festivals. I saw hundreds of thousands of people all at once as well as individual people doing specific acts like some kind of ritual. Like a floodgate was being opened, I saw an explosion of the entire drug culture being released. I saw people openly doing deadly things with drugs and needles.

As I gazed at this, I was mostly in observer mode, and some of what I was being shown moved rapidly and progressively before me. Yet some of the people and events were magnified and intensified as I sank into the matrix of the vision—a spiritual close-up. I watched three people closely related to me exit a familiar car, and then suddenly I was standing face-to-face with one of them. I perceived that they were severely dulled by drugs and unreachable. Overwhelmed by compassion, I wanted to help, but I could not get through to them because of the power of the drug effect.

As various scenes moved in chronological progression, some of them caused me to have compassion and others concerned me because of the negative chain of events that I knew would follow. Strangely, I cared strongly about things that had not yet come to pass. Also, my involvement in some of the sequences I was seeing concerned me as I told myself from an observer's viewpoint, "This shouldn't be going on. I should not be associated with these things."

Another close-up scene took place as I saw myself walking past an old-fashioned house and then down a pathway leading to a rusty gate. As the gate swung open I saw and smelled lilac bushes. I felt the warmth of the sun and heard the squeaking of the gate. There was an overwhelming feeling of peace and pleasantness. In a gentle but powerful way, I knew this was significant. Then I saw the face of a beautiful young blonde girl with a sweet smile. This was Barbara, my future wife, at our first home—a little farm in Ohio where we would raise horses, have children, and begin our lives together. All of this was going to happen more than five years in the future. But it was so real I felt I was really there. How could I smell flowers, feel the warmth of the sun, and hear sounds? I had no physical body with five senses, no eyes with nerves going to my brain to process sight.

Multiple living scenes flowed by, and another one was intensified. I saw myself standing on the beach in a beautiful, tropical place. I was facing a man with long braided hair. He was shaking a twisted branch with his left hand and squeezing lemon onto his hair with his right hand. He stared at me and chanted something. Between my two feet was a dry piece of driftwood. An overwhelming sense of evil emanated from this man. I turned 180 degrees and ran as fast as I could toward the setting sun, seemingly forever.

Then I saw myself walking with a small group of people down from a beautiful, tropical hilltop. I saw close-ups of every kind of flower, tropical fruit, and exotic tree, as well as a crystal stream flowing from the top of the hill into an idyllic emerald bay on the Caribbean sea. I observed clear close-ups of the people surveying the lush beauty of this property, smiling and laughing. Although I was observing this from a slight distance, I could hear the voice of one person saying, "So this is Paradise." I felt a peculiar wonder as I realized I was the one speaking and Barbara was walking next to me with a few other people. When I said the word *paradise,* the vision dissolved and I was again standing in the awesome presence of God.

He was communicating to me, but not in a verbal way or using any type of phonetic language. With a higher form of communication, pure Spirit revealed to me that I was being sent back to the world. My immediate response was feeling there was no way I wanted to leave the ecstasy of His glory and the intimacy of His love. But when the Lord speaks, it happens!

An invisible force gently drew me from the presence of the Lord, out of His radiant throne room, then through that mystical spirit realm I initially entered, and finally to the atmosphere of earth. Descending from the sky with my back to the earth, I penetrated the roof of the hospital, and my spirit sank into my physical body like a hand sliding into a glove. As this was happening, the ICU room materialized. The physical elements assimilated together much like the characters on Star Trek do when they are beamed up.

I lay flat on my back in the hospital bed, looking at the ceiling out of my left eye, and with my natural ears I heard myself thanking God with words and sayings completely unfamiliar to me, feeling literally beside myself during this ecstatic reentry. The young man condemned to death with multiple fatal complications was alive. More than alive, I was filled with electric love.

Although my body still had all the deadly symptoms and complications, I was overflowing with unnatural, incomprehensible peace. The Bible calls this "the peace of God, which surpasses all understanding."[9] Standing around my hospital bed were about a half dozen doctors and nurses. To my surprise I now had the ability to perceive and detect the soul and spirit of these human beings. They were clearly terrified. I could feel it individually and collectively—all their fear and confusion contrasting with their medical know-how.

Overwhelmed with compassion, I felt bad that *they* felt bad. I was never more secure, content, and protected. Before any physical change took place, I was amazingly comforted.

All this transcends logic, reason, and natural, physical, or psychological response. It was clearly *supernatural.* The clarity of the Father's love that I experienced while standing in His presence in heaven in the River of Life was not a distant remembrance of what had happened to me. God Himself and the river that I saw were actually *inside* of me.

The first direct communication I received from the Lord was an answer to my desperate prayer and feeble plea. He was giving me a second chance! Life is a precious, valuable gift. I was re-given the gift of life. Eternal life had already begun and everything about my was about to change…forever.

Fifteen

Dawn of a New Day

Hidden mysteries remain unseen, but mysteries that are revealed belong to the recipient.

Awaking in my devastated but revived physical body was a contradiction of normal. Normally when a person experiences something new and powerfully dramatic, they mentally demand to understand. I was saturated in an all-encompassing peace that is unlike anything earthly. With a radiant inner presence and a radically new state of being, I was beyond caring about mentally investigating something so emotionally transforming.

The intense pain was full on, but the rattling fever subsided. I'm sure the doctors gave me the maximum allowable painkiller and were still waiting for me to die. But there was a Power stronger than death inside me and I survived the night.

For well over a week leading up to this point, every time the nurse brought my meal tray in, I ate my food and immediately it spewed out of my mouth. The medical team presumed I had lost the will to live so I was throwing up all my food. The surgeon ordered a portable X-ray machine into ICU to examine my gastrointestinal tract. To the doctors' amazement my esophagus had been damaged by stomach acid while I was in the coma, creating a stricture closing three inches long leading into my stomach, barely wide enough for water to pass through. On top of everything else, I was dying of starvation!

With nothing else to lose, they performed a major surgical procedure, cutting all the way to my stomach and inserting a gastrostomy tube. They mixed protein shakes with liquid vitamins and medicine in a blender, then put it in a suspended medical bag, feeding it directly into my stomach three times a day. This procedure gives a whole new meaning to the term *bag lunch*! As I absorbed the nutrients, my body began to respond. With strength ebbing into my system, the infections stopped killing me. The doctors removed the pure oxygen line as my breathing capacity increased and my rigid chest loosened. The tide was turning.

It is amazing how our bodies function.

As alertness and clarity returned, the pain got worse. I also became aware that there were other serious physical problems. I had developed massive bedsores. The tissue on both of my heels was completely worn away, exposing the bones. My left hip had a four-inch opening showing the pointy part of my pelvis. Another six-inch area of my backside was completely raw, with bare tissue.

Decubitus ulcers (bedsores) are caused by pressure from unsupported body weight. They close off the capillaries and blood vessels that supply life-giving blood to our bodies, then the tissue begins to die and decay. Because I was in a coma and presumably dying, the doctors did not give me any treatment to prevent these sores from developing.

Though I was still considered critical and unstable, the head doctor resumed aggressive treatment. He brought a household scale into ICU, picked me up in his arms, and stood on the scale. After subtracting my weight from his, he gently laid me back in my bed and said, "Ninety-eight pounds." His smile told the tale: game on. Something he didn't understand was going on and he was going to cooperate with it.

A week or so after the crash, my mom's brother offered to pay to fly me to Brooke Hospital in Texas—a state-of-the-art burn center where Vietnam soldiers were treated for burns. Doctors warned that I'd never survive the trip. But at least I knew there was a ray of hope.

Hope is misunderstood and greatly undervalued. As I became more alert, I realized that I had been getting large numbers of get-well cards every day from people who were hoping, against all odds, for the impossible. (Years later, I learned about the massive prayer and selfless encounters people were having on my behalf. They were standing before God, between me and death, pleading my case and asking for mercy.)

When Julie came to visit, I was more emotionally engaged and intentional with her about our relationship than I had been before the accident. Also, for the first time, I was sensitive to how people were responding to me. On one occasion I reached up with the only part of my body that somewhat worked: my left hand. I grabbed Julie's coat and pulled her close so she could kiss me goodbye somewhere on my face that wasn't damaged. I could sense her internal conflict.

Most of the times that she had visited me, I was only partially conscious. Now that my thoughts and memory were working, I told her, "When I get out of here, I'm really getting into shape. I am going to work out and build up to about a hundred and eighty-five pounds."

"Oh, Mickey, don't worry about that," she said. "I want you just the way you are."

Her response made me feel funny. There was no going back to the way I was. I realize now that she was just trying to face reality. However, at the time, I didn't feel that way. Nor was I aware of what this situation was like for her.

It was time for her to get back to college, having missed so much already. I was okay with her doing that. I trusted her and the decision. My love for her was one of the few things that didn't get scarred. And Julie wrote me beautiful cards every day, with loving and thoughtful words written in perfect penmanship.

One day I overheard one of the doctors speaking sharply to a nurse, and the sound of his words made me cringe. For some reason, I had become extraordinarily sensitive.

When a person's physical activity is sharply reduced, the five senses commonly become enhanced. But this was different. I could feel their emotions and even anticipate their forthcoming thoughts. It wasn't mind reading; it was my inner being cooperating with the Spirit of God. Even the slightest expression of conflict caused me to have compassion without judging the offense, and feel remorseful that this negative thing had happened to them.

Love changes how we see everything. You don't have to look for the good in people. A love-transformed heart perceives it automatically. I couldn't help myself loving everybody and everything, which was quite abnormal for me.

I once commented to a visitor about how pretty a black singing group appeared on a magazine cover. This stately woman who was close to our family said, "Yes, she is…for a colored person." It seemed odd to me that she said that instead of just agreeing on the singer's beauty. Racism wasn't even a thought in my mind; it had been eradicated by supernatural love. I no longer looked *at* people. I could see *into* people…and they are all magnificent.

A small housefly landed on the chrome safety rail on the side of my hospital bed. I marveled at how intricate its eyes were and how the color refracted through its transparent wings. I remember thinking, *Hey, you can come visit me anytime. You are so incredible.*

Dan Harding never missed a day visiting me. Observing my tiny improvement, he brought me a *Playboy* magazine, thinking it would perk me up. When I kindly said I wasn't interested, he asked my sister, "Is Mickey religious?"

"No, not at all," she said matter-of-factly. I hadn't consciously processed this decision to say no to Dan's gift. I was simply living a different kind of life.

Dr. Nick ordered that I start therapy. The first whirlpool bath treatment was dramatic. During that plunge the water turned ghastly red as damaged, bloody tissue bubbled up to the surface. After three minutes, the physical therapist and the nurse lifted my ninety-eight-pound body and put me back into a wheelchair. I passed out instantly. When I woke up back in my bed, I felt reduced pain from the warm water and the whirlpool jets. That gave me something to look forward to every day, except for the passing-out part. The warm water started loosening my shrunken muscles and ligaments. Little things like that made a big difference.

A medical crisis broke out in the Intensive Care Unit. One of the patients, locked in a full-body cast from a car accident, developed a staph infection. If I'd caught that infection, it would have killed me. Like tearing down a battlefield MASH operation, the doctors quickly collected everything I needed and headed to the first floor. They set up a standard room to simulate intensive care, with all the IVs, machines, and temporary sanitary prepping. The beds were in an open area, with partitions for six patients.

One afternoon, as the volunteer candy striper was serving lunch, I asked the young girl if she had a mirror. She seemed hesitant, but took a small compact case out of her bag. I opened it and took a first look at my face. In the tiny reflection all I could see was that my right eye was wide open and both eyelids were completely retracted. I couldn't tell how disfigured I was, but her expression said it all. I thanked her and gave her back her mirror, deciding it was probably better that I didn't know.

Being revived did have some drawbacks. Dr. Nick drastically reduced my pain medication, and I went through morphine withdrawal. Thankfully, he allowed a strong pain shot in the morning for my bandage changing, which was a very painful two-hour process. In the evening I was allowed another injection to curb the pain so I could rest.

The addiction caused me to develop certain sensory attachments, like to the smell of the alcohol swab used to sterilize my skin. Like Pavlov's dog I connected that smell to relief. I didn't understand until much later how important it is to be free of negativity so I could respond to healing. The ecstatic love I received from God resulted in my tremendous transformation. However, as human beings, we are subject to our environment. As I woke up more to the natural world, I noticed a drastic difference in my awareness of conflicts and attitudes of those around me.

The caregivers on the first floor had mixed attitudes toward me. I was very difficult to take care of; it was an arduous task just changing my bandages. I was pretty helpless and very dependent. I was afraid some of the caregivers might think they were taking care of a lost cause. I was particularly afraid of one nurse who worked nights. She gave me ten pain shots during her eight-hour shift. I believe it was an attempt at a mercy killing. She was suddenly fired without explanation.

As I began to comprehend how catastrophic my injuries were, I cried out, "Why couldn't I have just broken my leg." Mentally and emotionally, the challenges seemed insurmountable. But by the grace of God I kept inching upward.

My new life had some high-water marks of spiritual help, best classified as a *power invasion.*

The first floor allowed access to more people than ICU did. One afternoon when I didn't have any visitors, a man walked into the room, walked right up to my bedside, and started praying for me. Then he asked if he could read me something from his Bible. That was a first. Nobody had ever asked that, nor had I ever seen anyone carrying a Bible. "Sure," I said. I was so weak that day, I had a hard time just turning my head to look at him.

As he read, something inside me shook my stomach muscles. He kept reading and that shaking grew stronger. It rose up like lava in a volcano. It became so strong my arms and legs were flapping like a person plugged in to high voltage. Sitting straight up I shouted, "I've got to be some kind of priest or something. I've been reborn."

Alarmed, my visitor said, "Just take it easy. Don't worry about that stuff now. Please calm down." He probably pictured tomorrow's headline: "Local Pastor Kills Helpless Burn Victim." He called for a nurse and ran out the door as fast as he could.

I had never heard the term *reborn*. Where did such power come from that shook me so violently and then enabled me to sit up? When the words he read from the Bible hit my ears, God's power rocked me and I said something that defined a "call" that was on my life. Jesus once said, "The kingdom is within you."[10] This power came from within me, but I wasn't born like this. This treasured encounter would have to remain a secret. How could I explain it, and who would understand?

A few weeks later Dr. Nick told me, "We've got to get you moving. I'm writing new orders for your physical therapy." My legs were extended straight out and rigid. My lifeless feet were like the claws of a dead bird, curled, with no movable response to stimuli.

While standing at the end of the bed with his hands against my feet, Dr. Nick pushed my legs so that my knees went to my chest. What a shock! All of my formerly fine tuned muscles had withered like little rubber bands and were stuck together in adhesions. I heard the muscles pop like snapping twine, and the sound was nothing compared to how it felt. Dr. Nick wasn't being cruel. Even though moving my legs was brutally painful, it was the right thing to do.

The next day I was taken to physical therapy. A nurse put a new pair of slippers on my feet, attached Velcro elastic straps over my toes, and rolled my wheelchair between parallel bars. A well-built physical therapist stood on my left and Dr. Nick on my right. They hoisted me up as I grabbed the bar with my left hand. I was standing! They were helping, but I was definitely standing.

As I dragged my right leg forward, followed by my left, the patchwork skin grafts on both legs tore, and rivulets of blood streamed down my legs. Two steps forward, two steps back, and *bam*, back down in the chair. I was ecstatic and exhausted. I felt like celebrating as if I'd stood on Mount Everest and won the Olympic gold at the same time. Do not despise the day of small beginnings!

The next morning I woke up with a new goal: "I'm gonna walk out of here." The same doctor that told my family I would never walk again helped make it happen.

Sparks of life became a small flame of light in the middle of my ocean of darkness.

I asked someone to bring me some art supplies. The side of my bed had sketchpads, various types of pencils, charcoals, and a clipboard. Having been artistic all my life, I was ready to go, except for one problem: I was right-handed. I'd never so much as dotted an *i* with my left hand. Amazingly, I drew one sketch after another, with beautiful likenesses perfectly proportioned. I drew things I'd never tried before—sketches of dogs, horses, buildings, and pristine landscapes. I couldn't sign my name to my creations. But all of my visitors crowded around the bed to gawk at my pictures, shocked by my ability to produce them. (That was before I heard about left-brain and right-brain functions.)

In therapy I used my hip flexors and thigh muscles to drag my legs a few steps back and forth between the parallel bars. The nerves and muscles from my knees down did not respond. I had what is called "bilateral foot drop." The elastic bands over the front of my slippers held them up because my legs could not.

Dr. Nick scheduled a test on the nervous system of my legs. The neurologist taped electrodes on various parts of my legs. The machine sent small electrical charges as he tested places of the nerve pathways of my legs. When he was done, he had a matter-of-fact, business-as-usual doctor look on his face.

That afternoon Dr. Nick came back to report the results. Point-blank in his honesty, he told me the tests concluded that my nerves were unresponsive. They were dead and would never return to usefulness. There was a tiny response at one point in my right leg, but it was negligible. The prognosis was that if I walked at all, I would require leg braces and probably crutches.

Rejecting that conclusion, I exploded with emotion. I declared with pretty colorful language, "I am going to walk without using any of that stuff!" I was engaged in a battle, determined to defeat any giant that might stand in my way. I did not know it then, but I found out later that the medical team had already told my family I would never walk again. But I was summoning strength and courage from a source beyond any human ability. In my weakness the strongest one was releasing power.

After my morning routine, the head nurse told me she had news of a change in my situation. "The doctors ordered you to be moved to Two West. That's on the second floor. The staff is organizing your room right now." Her tone was abrupt, almost like a military order.

After stripping down my little unit and moving all my stuff out of the room, two husky men rolled a hospital gurney alongside my bed. Then they and four nurses hoisted me up, sheet and all, onto the cart. They wheeled me down the hall, up the elevator, and around the corner into a new room. I felt like I'd been handed over to another jurisdiction.

Then she came in. "Hi, honey. I'm Mrs. Krucheck. I'll be taking care of you from now on." This woman in her mid to late fifties had such a radiant smile; *cheerful* would be a gross understatement. She had decorated the room in bright colors, and I had it all to myself. It seemed like a real improvement. (I found out later that the five rooms in this wing were reserved for hopeless cases. But this one human being was about to make a colossal impact on my life.)

When she removed the sheets to examine the lower part of my body, she stared at the bedsore damages of my heels, hip, and backside. "My Lord, what happened here?" She put a pillow under my ankles to suspend my feet off the bed. After carefully arranging my head pillow and blankets around me, she said quietly, "Just rest nicely. I'll be right back."

A short while later I heard Mrs. Krucheck engaged in a passionate conversation with the head nurse in charge of the Intensive Care Unit. The cheerful voice of my new caregiver was one notch below full-blown rage. "How could you people allow this to happen to this young man? There is absolutely no excuse for this damage. I'm making a full report of his condition and I will leave nothing out. Now, get out of my sight!"

I doubt my new nurse was aware that I could hear what was going on during that verbal machine-gunning.

About fifteen minutes passed and Mrs. Krucheck came back into my room with a cart full of supplies. She was even more cheerful than before as she gently unwrapped all the sticky, bloody bandages. She lovingly cleansed and applied antiseptic to all the wounds and open areas, which were the majority of my body. Using soft medicated gauze pads, she wrapped and cushioned my heels and bedsores on the other parts of my body._

Every day upon my return from the whirlpool treatment in physical therapy, she spent about two hours applying the bandages. This courageous woman memorized every part of my body, top to bottom, front and back, determined to bring healing to every little part that she could help. She was petite, about five feet tall, with the energy of an eighteen-year-old. When she entered my room, the atmosphere changed. It was more cheerful, like her.

Because my backside was almost completely raw, she ordered from therapy a Stryker pad to bring healing to my bedsores. She was always positive, and she told me, in detail, about the slightest improvement in the healing of my wounds. I was a lot a work to take care of, but this nurse acted like I was the only patient in the world. She was an authentic healer.

A deadly virus called the Hong Kong flu reached the United States. As a result, my room was in reverse quarantine. Anybody who visited me had to wear a long-sleeved surgical gown, gloves, mask, and head covering. Visitors never stopped coming to see me, and most of them left sweaty and hot underneath all that stuff.

My legs and muscles were coming alive, and the pain was intensifying. I asked almost everyone who visited me, "Could you please squeeze my legs?" I felt bad for them. Part of me was bandaged like a mummy, and the other part of me was naked and probably difficult to look at. But they helped. Their touches not only relieved my pain, I am convinced that their sacrificial giving released the power of *wake-up life* to my dead limbs.

My fourteen-year-old brother, Robert, was the most faithful of all of my caregivers. He rearranged his schedule to get out of school at noon, and every day he walked or hitchhiked to the hospital. He sat beside me hour after hour, gently squeezing my legs. He never gave up on me, and his commitment was one of the sparks that kindled life back into my broken, withered body. If it wasn't for him, I think I would have died.

Whether they knew it or not, all of my caregivers were healers.

One day I told my nurse, "Hey, I think I'm starting to see out of my right eye." In fifteen minutes I was under anesthesia in surgery. The damaged tissue on my right eye was thinning out and my eye was about to explode. The eye specialist put a donor cornea graft from a cadaver on my eye, and a plastic surgeon made eyelids from the back of my left ear. My eye had to be sewn shut for six weeks. The goal was just to save the eye, not to restore sight. Twice a day the eye specialist put medication on the area. He was concerned that infection would start and spread to the other eye, making me blind in both.

Six weeks later the stitches were taken out, the crisis was over, and the good guys won. My right eye was still blind, but it was intact thanks to the donated cornea from the eye bank. God does indeed work through the hands of doctors, nurses, and medicine.

My daily therapy incorporated a whirlpool bath, including a full box of Dreft diaper soap in the water. I wonder who thought that would be good? After lunch, I headed to the parallel bars, the Velcro straps holding up my drop foot as I made my Frankenstein-like walk forward, then backward, then sat down in the chair and passed out. Ever so gradually the upper parts my legs grew stronger. Until I got sick.

I didn't catch the Hong Kong flu, but I had uncontrollable vomiting until there was nothing left in me. Good friends came to see me, and I was embarrassed when they tried to comfort me, knowing how uncomfortable it must have been for them. Two good friends from school, Cliff and Kathy, visited on one of my worst days. I'll always remember their encouragement to never give up.

Dr. Nick and Mrs. Kruchek informed me that they were trying to get me admitted to a rehabilitation hospital called Highland View on the east side of Cleveland. It sounded like kind of a Mayo Clinic for the hopelessly disabled. It had all the equipment, surgery, and therapy I needed, including a huge whirlpool called the Hubbard Tank. It sounded severe, but they assured me it would be good for somebody in my condition.

I had to wait for a space to open up. During that time I became so weak I was unable to walk. I attributed that to spiritual warfare. Evil forces really do battle against the good destiny and welfare of God's people. To have miraculously gained the power to walk, as feeble as it was, was a miracle. The idea of losing that miracle was beyond unbearable and had the greatest potential for discouragement.

On Christmas Eve, 1968, the world watched Apollo 8 go into lunar orbit. The crew consisted of astronauts Frank Borman, William A. Anders, and James A. Lovell of Apollo 13 fame. When they disappeared into the dark side of the moon, the largest television audience ever—including me—held their breath. There was complete radio silence for more than thirty minutes. Nobody knew if the spacecraft would crash into the moon or sling off irretrievably into outer space and kill the astronauts.

When they came around from the backside of the moon, the first voice to speak said, "In the beginning God created the heaven and the earth. And the earth was without form, and void; and darkness was upon the face of the deep. And the Spirit of God moved upon the face of the waters. And God said, Let there be light: and there was light. And God saw the light, that it was good: and God divided the light from the darkness. And God called the light Day, and the darkness he called Night. And the evening and the morning were the first day."[11]

I burst out crying, not with tears of sadness and discouragement but tears of hope. Hope because years earlier President John F. Kennedy made an astounding faith declaration that the United States of America would send men to the moon and bring them back to earth safely. Being an avid student of aeronautical science,

I knew this was all but impossible, especially after the disastrous fire and death of three astronauts in a rehearsal for Apollo 1.

Hope is not some whimsical wish that maybe something might happen. It is an explosive expectation that something miraculous *will* happen. And as I wept with joy, hope exploded inside my spirit and resonated through my entire being. These concepts were not in my mind and I didn't possess the words to say them, but the Spirit of God inside me was the hope explosion that caused this incredible response.

My hope is in the Lord.

On January 20, 1969, I was released from Southwest Community Hospital in Berea, Ohio, after a little over five months. This was the same hospital I visited four days before the crash where I said, "I could never stand one night in a dreary place like this." Ironic. Strange. No, I don't understand everything. Although I hadn't regained enough strength to walk out, I had the strength within me to press on.

The ambulance took me with my mother and my brother to our house in Parma Heights, Ohio. The Christmas tree was still up, and it looked as sick I was, but I was glad to be home. When they rolled me in on the cart, it might as well been Buckingham Palace. There is no place like home, be it ever so humble.

They'd fixed my room up with all the medical jazz to hold me up for eight hours until the ambulance took me to Highland View. Family and a few friends popped in to see me *not* in a hospital. There was a tremendous sense of belonging and well wishing. Coming home for a day was medically pretty risky, but some risk is involved in healing.

The next day the ambulance carried me to my new residence in Highland View, a four-hundred-bed hospital designed for double amputees, quadriplegics, people with head injuries, and worse. Some patients stayed for many months. Others didn't make it.

The doctor allowed my mom and Robbie to go with me into the examining room that first day. I hadn't taken any medication yet, so when the nurse started to remove my bandages, I went ballistic from the pain. I was so wracked up I failed to see the look on my mom's face. She'd never seen my unbandaged body before. I vaguely heard her screaming hysterically, "Oh, my God! What have you done to him? What have you done to him?"

The nurses removed her from the room to calm her down. I think the Lord had somehow blinded my mother from seeing how horrible my injuries really were. She's the only one who never believed I would die. Robbie, who knew me better than anybody at that point, told me later, "You looked like you got in another plane crash on the way to the hospital."

I was put in a large room with three other patients. At my right was Bob, a law student paralyzed from the neck down from a car accident. Straight across from me was Roy, a redneck paralyzed from the waist down as result of a gunshot. In the other corner was Larry, a black man who was a quadriplegic after breaking his neck in a minor car accident. Then there was me: former athlete, former stock trader, former skydiver.

Only the strangest twist of fate could have made roommates out of a redneck, a black man, a law student, and a skydiver. In day-to-day life at that time in history, we would have nothing in common, but in there with broken bodies, we were alive and we had each other. I'd say we were the dream team!

My roommates were as alive as anyone I'd ever known, yet five months previously, if I'd seen any of them, I would have looked the other way. Before my accident, I never knew places like Highland View existed.

People need life from the outside as much as plants need sunlight, and since I was blessed with many visitors, I gladly shared the wealth with my roommates. They quickly adopted my friends and family.

The physical therapy doctor figured out that the only way I could be comfortable would be to use a medical waterbed. It was a rectangular foam mattress with a vinyl insert filled with water. The surface equally distributed my weight, giving my sores a better chance to heal.

Right away they scheduled a week of physical therapy evaluations. It was like Gold's Gym for the really handicapped. It had mats, pulleys, wedges, weights, and gadgets to help the helpless. I think this staff of therapists invented the phrase "No pain, no gain." My plan had something different every morning and afternoon, five days a week.

The hospital included every kind of clinic for the teeth, eyes, diet, orthopedics, and equipment for any type of surgical situation. Since I had something wrong with me in all those categories, I really got around. They also had speech therapy—the only place I didn't have to go to. Being moved around so much helped me redevelop my social skills. I had to show up on time, follow orders, and try to do whatever I could for myself, which wasn't much.

The specialty at this place was physical therapy. I was like a classic car found in a barn, rusted solid and half sunk in the mud. I needed therapy for every muscle, connective tissue, joint, and fiber to get this clunker running. The severe scarring was restricting my range of motion in several areas. I could not move my right arm more than six inches from the side of my hip. The whole right side of my body, including my shoulder, neck, and more than half of my face, was scarred and tight like dried leather. I couldn't move my head from right to left, so I could only look straight ahead. There were still a lot of open wounds on my heels, my right hand, and some of the patchwork area of the skin grafts.

The Whirlpool was a giant T-shaped tank with four strong agitators to propel warm water over the patient. Every day I was placed on a stretcher, lifted up with a chain hoist, and lowered into the water. The water was never warm enough for me. I kept asking the therapist to take it up a few degrees. After pushing my withered feet upward, she tried to straighten each toe individually. The combination of the warm water and hands-on movement relieved the intense pain and stiffness from six months of rigor mortis. I always told her to keep doing that part a little more. "You just want a massage, don't you?" she said with a smile. There were a lot of other people she had to take care of it, and I really did appreciate her work ethic with me.

Another therapist worked on my range of motion to get that arm to move more than six inches. A husky therapist got the assignment of getting me up between some big parallel bars in a room full of mirrors. It was the same kind of rig I'd used before to get myself to stand and walk again. But this time I had to push a little harder every day and with every therapy.

When I looked in the mirror, I saw how skinny and withered I was. With my head and hand bandaged heavily, a black plastic patch over my right eye, and the hospital gown hanging on my bony body, I was quite a sight to see.

Every day, the physical therapists unwrapped me from my bandages. I felt like Lazarus from the Bible, who, after being raised from the dead, was still wrapped in grave clothes. At first Lazarus was alive, but limited. I had already transcended some of life's most impossible horrors. What were my limitations now?

Mickey, left, had an early interest in aviation.

Starting school.

Senior picture during the stockbroker days.

Mickey lands with his Para-Commander parachute in early spring of 1968.

Aftermath of the tragic crash of August 15, 1968.

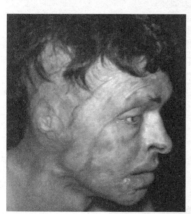

Still badly burned and hanging onto life, December 1968.

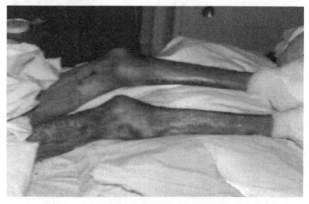

Both legs paralyzed with severe nerve damage.

One small step for Mickey, one giant leap of hope for a miraculous recovery!

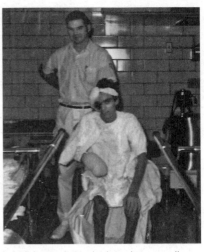

With my therapist learning to walk.

In the hospital.

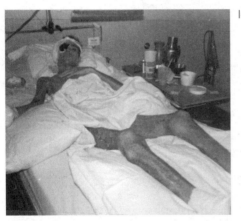

In the hospital with one of my nurses.

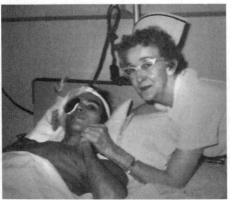

At the Bay of Fundy, New Brunswick, Canada. I climbed to the top of the famous 60-foot rock formation with a friend. (Left)

A close-up as proclaimed by Psalm 40:2: "He set my feet on a rock, and gave me a firm place to stand." (Right) You can see how big the rock formation is we climbed.

Skiing in the Austrian Alps.

Mickey and Barbara

Sixteen

Ashes to Gold

Six months without taking any nourishment by mouth is a long fast by anybody's standards. My food—a high-protein mix with vitamins and some medicine—was mixed in a blender then put in a bag that hung above my bed. The nourishment went through a tube about a quarter inch in diameter and then drained into my stomach.

A group of doctors analyzed my X-rays and discovered that my esophagus was the normal size except for the last three and a half inches, which had been scarred to a thin stricture, allowing only a watery substance to pass through. The doctors explained to me their plan to try to expand the opening.

In preparation for my first surgery at Highland View, as I lay on the surgical table, the doctors made me swallow a numbing substance called Xylocaine viscous. They told me it was supposed to make the surgery painless. I had to hang my head off the back of the table as they pushed some type of optic scope down my throat through the tiny opening and into my stomach. I felt like I had swallowed Mel Gibson's *Braveheart* sword! Then fifteen medical students took turns looking down the scope.

A doctor with a light on his head fished around the hole in my belly, looking for a string that had been run down the scope into my stomach. He pulled it out and taped it to my side. Another doctor fed the other end of the string out my left nostril. When it was time to stretch my esophagus, they moved the string (which looked like waxed dental floss) from my nostril into my mouth, tied a tiny stainless steel bullet around the end, and pulled on the end of the string coming out of my stomach and belly to make the bullet go down my throat, stretching my esophagus ever so slightly.

This procedure was done every Tuesday and Thursday. They let me swallow the numbing stuff every time, but I had to be awake. Although the Xylocaine numbed my tongue, the back of my mouth, and my throat (except at the scarred part), I felt like somebody was pulling a football through me. This was painless?

After four treatments in two weeks, I ate five bowls of liquefied mashed potatoes with butter and salt. It might as well have been steak and lobster! Little by little I grew stronger and gained weight.

The third week I tried cream of celery soup with salt. I liked salt. I started to feel like a real person. Every day I was making progress, and every day the three men in my room celebrated my little victories.

Because my right hand couldn't do anything, I was given a special wheelchair with two rims on the left side that allowed me to steer with one hand. I finally had mobility, at least a little…as much as I could take sitting down. I didn't keep track of my progress; I just kept going. I had visitors every day and every night, and they noticed whenever I gained even a little momentum.

One day without any announcement, my father showed up in the middle of the afternoon. With his hand on my bed's guard rail, he looked at me and said, "Hi, Son. I just took a chance that you wouldn't mind seeing me. I thought it would be…" His voice quivered and he coughed to clear his throat. "Just a second. I'll be right back." He walked out of my room and disappeared down the hall.

Several minutes later, he came back and walked up to the side of my bed again. I could tell he'd been crying. I had never seen my dad shed a tear or show any sorrowful emotions, except when he got misty-eyed the day he found out his mother had died.

I started crying from down deep inside me. "Dad," I said, "why does it have to be like this?" Under all of my hurt and resentment, I loved my dad and I knew he loved me.

"I've done everything wrong," he said, emotion choking his voice. "All the drinking, all the trouble in our family. I made a mess of my life. But you're young, and you've always tried to do your best. How could this happen to you? I don't understand."

With his tears came complete forgiveness and reconciliation. We never discussed any details or asked for any explanation. All of the tension between us was simply wiped clean. Years of intense conflict and escalating hostilities that left me full of toxic memories and emotions were all washed away with cleansing tears coming from both me and my father. And those inner wounds did not leave scars like the fiery plane crash did on my body.

I didn't understand what the Bible teaches about forgiveness. All I can say is that forgiveness worked a miracle that neither my father nor I was capable of on our own.

I learned later that if we want God to forgive our offenses, we must be willing to forgive others. I also learned the immense power of these words: "Blessed are the merciful, for they shall obtain mercy."[12] Holding on to unforgiveness is like being locked in a jail cell made out of bars of bitterness.

My father didn't change the things in his lifestyle that I didn't like. But I was free concerning our relationship, and so was he. Inner healing of damaged emotions is sometimes connected to healing of damaged bodies.

Years later, before he died, my stone-cold atheistic father found peace with God and put his trust in the Lord Jesus Christ.

My skydiving buddy Jerry was going to Florida for a week of free fall training while it was freezing in Ohio. He asked Robert to go with him. Robert was part of a group of three underage guys we called "the flying punks." They were the youngest skydivers in America. Robert had not missed one day of seeing me since August 15. But I encouraged him to go, knowing he would love it.

Jerry and Robert went to Florida, and Jerry picked up the tab for everything. My little brother had the time his life with a good friend. I was overjoyed that Robert was getting rewarded with something he could never do on his own.

The day before they got back, I was having a skin-graft operation. These procedures had become common routine for me. I knew I would hurt, but I would get over it. But this time, for some reason, something went wrong. The anesthetic was too strong, my blood pressure plummeted, and I was unconscious all day and well into the night. Just before dawn I heard a whispering sound. "Mr. Robinson, can you hear me?" I woke up and realized that person was actually screaming in my ear. I almost died from that overdose. I never talked to anybody about it; I was just glad they were able to bring me back.

The next day Jerry brought Robert to the hospital to see me. They came alongside my bed and my brother said, "So, what have you been doing while we were gone?"

I replied, "I guess I made a real *ash* out of myself." Burn-crash pun. They burst out laughing with surprise and relief.

Humor is part of healing, and that was the first spontaneously funny thing I'd ever said. This was a good sign. Scripture says, "A merry heart does good, like medicine."[13]

I was happy to hear the stories about their skydiving trip, especially Robert's. They had a blast.

The doctors determined I could get away from the hospital for an eight-hour outing on a Saturday. Robert and Jimmy, who also lived in our house and helped out by providing transportation, picked me up on a Saturday morning. Eight hours was about as long as I could take, but it was good to get outside of the hospital and actually go into a house.

After a couple of these outings, my friends and family found amusement by imitating me trying to walk the way I did in therapy. They did a good look-alike of me, going in slow motion like a gooney bird trying to take off. I wasn't very good at chasing them in my wheelchair, so I threw my crutches at them. Men will be boys, and I think playing is also part of healing.

The hospital had an art studio for their patients that was developed by a young woman named Micki McGraw. She was in a wheelchair, but she was a mover and a shaker. I visited the studio and began doing art left-handed. I made a beautiful mountain scene with a lake and pine trees—a quiet, serene pen-and-ink drawing.

Word got out, and someone from the Cleveland newspaper came, took a picture of me and my art, and put it in the paper. Art is therapeutic, and I believe creativity is another part of healing.

My friends Grant and Linda, with whom Julie and I always double dated, were getting married in a month, so I etched their initials in a rock that was part of the drawing, then gave it to them as a wedding present.

One day the nurse came into my room and said, "You have a phone call. You can pick it up on the pay phone at the nurse's station." It was about seven o'clock in the evening.

She wheeled me to the nurse's station, and I picked up the receiver. "This is Mickey."

"Hi. It's Julie. I'm calling from school." It was just to hear her voice. I hadn't seen her since Christmas, although she wrote every day. After a pause, she said, "Mickey, I've given this a lot of thought, and I just don't think we have a future together."

"What are you saying?"

"I'm sorry, Mickey. But I'm sure about this. It's best for you too. I've got to go now."

I could hardly breathe. I held the phone to my left ear until it made a busy signal. I hung up and looked down the hall, which was as empty as my heart.

I was devastated. Julie was the only thing I had left of my former life, and our wedding was what I had to look forward to for the future. I knew I needed to talk to somebody, but I wasn't ready and I didn't know whom I could talk to. So I rolled slowly past my room to a dark place at the end of the hall, where I tried to pull myself together. I didn't want the guys to know what had happened.

Finally I rolled the wheelchair back to my room. The nurse helped me into bed and gave me my eight o'clock medicine. I turned to the wall, staring at nothing. *How could this happen?* I couldn't sleep.

About three a.m. I started to sob from deep within. I did my best to bury it in the pillow. But within a few minutes I heard a voice. "Man, you're going to be all right. They're gonna fix you up. You'll be back on the street doin' yer thing in no time. Nothin's gonna stop you, man. Nothin'." It was Larry, my paralyzed, black roommate. As Larry's words moved across the dark room, I felt waves of love hitting me like breakers smacking the beach. Each word carried the love of the Father. It was the same vibration of love I'd felt in heaven, the same love that sent me back to earth.

With each word my sobs receded, and when he stopped speaking, there was no more weeping. This comfort came from a man paralyzed from the neck down who did not know what Julie had said to me on the phone. God used him as an instrument to "bind up the brokenhearted." Only God can make beauty from ashes.

The next morning after breakfast and before therapy, I rolled my wheelchair next to Larry's bed frame and put my left hand on his shoulder. " I really love you, man. Thank you. I mean it. You did it for me."

I went down to therapy and hit it as hard as I could. I kept hearing Larry's voice saying, "Nothin's gonna stop you, man. Nothin'." Every time the therapist stretched my muscles, I felt God's love comforting me.

After that day, my progress really accelerated. I got stronger and gained a little weight. I tried walking outside of the parallel bars. The therapist gave me a four-pronged aluminum cane that I could hold with my left hand. It was a little scary, but I did it and actually I did really well. The therapist fitted my legs for braces from my knees down. They looked like Charlie Chaplin black shoes and kept my feet from dropping down. They gave me greater balance, and I used them more and more.

When Dan, my skydiving partner, first saw me walk with the quad-cane, that tough guy cried like a baby. It was his victory too. He had pulled me from the burning airplane. He never let me speak negatively. He came to see me almost every day. And finally he saw me walk!

I had the esophagus-stretching procedure twice a week. And I had other operations, like skin grafting. I may have had more stitches than all the baseballs in the Cleveland Indians dugout. The operations hurt, but at least I wasn't sick anymore. Therapy was canceled on the days I had surgery. And I had quite a supporting cast of family, visitors, and my three roommates—the dream team.

Three weeks after the phone call from Julie, I heard a loud crash. I pulled the string to turn on my light. Larry had metal tongs stuck into holes on either side of his head and a cord going through a pulley that held about fifty pounds of weight, which held his neck in place as the bone graft was healing his broken spinal column. Somehow the tongs had pulled out of his head!

With no time to get in a wheelchair, I threw myself on the

floor. I dragged myself across the room, pulled myself up with my left hand, and with my bandaged right hand, I held his head steady. As his blood flowed through the fingers on my left hand, I screamed, "Nurse! Get in here right now!"

I knew that paralyzed people can move from involuntary muscle spasms. If Larry were to have a spasm and his head fell off the pad, he would be dead. I literally held his life in my hands, just as he had held mine in his three weeks previously. Thankfully, the nurse and surgeon came in to put the metal tongs back in his head.

Three weeks before Grant and Linda's wedding, my therapist and the doctors agreed that I could get a pass to attend the ceremony. I signed all kinds of papers saying that if anything happened, it was their fault. Somebody found me some pants, a decent dress shirt, a tie, and a sport jacket. I was really thin, but about eighteen pounds more than when I arrived and incredibly stronger. The nurses helped me get into the clothes, carefully pulling my pants over the leg brace and my Charlie Chaplin-like shoes. Then they combed what was left of my hair. I was ready to go.

My sister's good friend Sandy picked me up in her GTO. Because I was really late, she put the pedal to the metal. We got to St. Michael's Church, the one I grew up in, after the wedding had started. With Sandy's help, I made it up the stairs. We went in the door and sat in the back row. Nobody saw me.

It was hard for my bony bottom to sit that long on a wooden church pew. But I was glad I made it to see this. Especially since Julie was the maid of honor.

When the minister pronounced Grand and Linda husband and wife, the whole church stood and watched the bride and groom happily walk down the aisle. When Grant saw me, he stopped in his tracks. The people behind him crashed into his back. When everybody saw me, they all ran over to hug me, except Julie. She smiled and walked right past me.

At the reception, I visited with all my old friends and their girlfriends and family members. Julie came over and bent down to give me a peck on the cheek. She said, "You look really good, Mickey." When she said that, I knew it was over between us. My former life was gone.

I didn't stay as long as everybody else. The event was emotionally tiring and physically painful. Still, I was grateful for all the people who made it possible for me to unwrap this particular part of my grave clothes.

As Sandy drove me back to the hospital, I felt like a man without a country. All that had once mattered to me was gone. The old Mickey Robinson was dead. He died in that plane crash, and he wasn't coming back. But I was determined to meet the man who would take his place. I didn't know anything about psychology, but I felt like I had to let go of the past so I could find my future.

My treatment advanced to putting real food in a blender. The dilation process, making my scarred esophagus a little wider, increased to every Tuesday and Thursday. I had a green string permanently sticking out of my left nostril, with the other end in my stomach. At night I wrapped the string around a tongue depressor and put a bunch of tape over it on my face.

On the days I had that procedure and no official physical therapy, I did my own exercising in my room with tiny weights, sandbags, and some pulleys rigged up at the end of my bed frame.

The last part of my routine was to sit on the bed and speak to my legs. I'd say, "Come on, legs, move!" Gradually my right leg started to move a little. The therapists and doctors remarked about it, but they didn't think much would come from it. The nerves had been dead for a long time. My main therapist told me to get used to wearing the leg brace because I would need it for the rest of my life.

One Thursday, I was scheduled for another round of swallowing the bullet down my throat. Twenty minutes before the session, I was sitting on the bed after my workout, telling my legs, "I want you to move. Come on, now, move!"

Instantaneously my left leg was completely restored. I could move my foot and ankle, and I had feeling where I had not previously. I stood up without the cane and started walking around in circles. I grabbed the buzzer and started screaming for the doctors and nurses. When they came running into the room, I hollered, "Look at this! Look what I can do! They're working!"

I didn't know anything about divine healing. I didn't know what the Bible said about it. All I knew was that I had been lame and now I could walk. This was a real, authentic, creative miracle.

My roommates went crazy. The nurses were scared. They still took me down for the procedure, putting a bigger bullet down my throat. But I didn't care. I got my legs back! From that moment, I knew I would never wear leg braces again.

After this miracle, my primary care doctor, who was studying to become a plastic surgeon, took me to every one of the clinics in his hospital. He told the other doctors, "I did a new procedure today. Watch this." He pulled the string from my nose and I kicked my leg up. All of the medical people in that hospital knew I could only walk with leg braces. And now, I was walking unassisted. This miracle was golden.

God once said to Moses, "Is there any limit to my power?"[14] I felt like asking the same question. I had just experienced an incredible and miraculous milestone. To have the nerves in my leg dead for nearly one year and then spring to life in one moment transcends all thresholds of natural law.

(Many years later, in a magazine interview, the editors asked a neurologist and rehabilitation specialist about my case. He said that in thirty-three years of practice, he had never seen a sudden restoration of nerves like mine. He stated the underlying nerve fibers would have to respond to therapy, which would be long and limited. Based on his medical knowledge, he said he would not hesitate to use the term *miracle*.)

This caused me to push even harder in therapy. I did more than the therapist asked. I began eating regular food—well, kind of regular. It was soft stuff that was ground up enough to get down past the scar tissue. And I stopped wearing hospital clothing.

The surgeon took the tube out of my stomach and said the hole would just close itself up and heal over time.

The gastrointestinal doctor came to see me. He said, "We've done about as much as we can do stretching out your esophagus. Your diet will be the full spectrum of food, but in softened form. And you'll need your esophagus dilated about twice a year for the rest of your life." He described how they would use an instrument to expand that portion of scar tissue and that it would have a tendency to shrink little by little.

He officially took himself off the case. He had done his job. That left me feeling confused, like he had just told me I was never going to be normal.

I'd heard that some of the patients gathered in the cafeteria on Sunday mornings to celebrate Mass with the chaplain. So I attended for the first time, hanging in the back. In front of me were people in gurneys and wheelchairs, all listening to the Catholic liturgy in Latin. I really paid attention, and afterward I stayed to say hi to the priest and ask if he would come up and give me ashes on Ash Wednesday, which was that week.

This guy was different from the priests I grew up with. He smiled a lot and made jokes, and he did not wear the usual priestly robe. He wore an ordinary plaid shirt with a one-inch strip of starched white cloth between his collars.

He came to my room that Wednesday. "You don't really need to do this. I don't think it's good to focus on death."

But I still wanted the ashes, maybe just because I'd done it all my life. I had intended talk to him about the phone call from Julie. But although he was very friendly, I just couldn't connect with him.

I pressed harder into my therapy. My right arm had been stretched as high as parallel to the ground when I was standing. But I couldn't raise it over my head. My forearm was frozen. I couldn't turn it over and it wouldn't pronate or supinate. One day I grabbed my right wrist with my left hand, gritted my teeth, and turned it until I heard a loud *snap*. That action increased the rotation, so I kept stretching everything a little farther each time until I had complete mobility in that arm.

Recovery became my full-time job, and I threw myself into it with passion. My right hand finally started to recover from all the wounds, but it wasn't very useful. I couldn't hold anything with it. I had a little movement between what was left of my thumb and forefinger. In occupational therapy I had to learn how to do everything with my left hand: buttoning my shirt, putting on pants, tying my shoes with one hand—that was a tough one. Other patients told me they would rather lose a leg than an arm or hand.

I began to feel that the therapists were trying to prepare me to be a handicapped person for the rest of my life. They were being realistic, and some of them had taken me as far as they thought I could reach. But I wasn't interested in having a handicap.

The art studio was one of the most positive places at Highland View Hospital. Micki McGraw was always playing the latest rock music and singing along with it. As I sat in the studio making pictures of the South Sea Islands, palm trees, or snowcapped mountain peaks, I found myself dreaming—seeing myself skiing down the mountains and sailing around the islands. I didn't know it then, but vision and imagination are steps of faith. Somewhere deep inside I was yearning to make a connection here on earth with the Majesty I'd experienced in heaven, but I didn't know where or how.

One sunny Saturday morning, I was eating my breakfast when Dan Harding and my brother bolted through the door. "You're coming with us, man," Robert said. "You're in for a surprise." They loaded me into the car and headed in the opposite direction from my house.

"Where are you taking me?" I asked.

They didn't answer.

We got onto a country road I knew well. Dan left a cloud of dust on the gravel road and pulled right up to the skydiving airplane. The plane owner said he would allow me to come along if I promised not to jump out of the plane. I was elated!

I got into the plane with Dan. As I mentally prepared myself for my first flight after the crash, I thought, *If I'm going to be spooked, it'll probably be at takeoff.* But when the Cessna took off, it was like my accident had never happened.

At ten thousand feet, the door opened. Dan gave me a thumbs-up, then disappeared. I stuck my head out a little in the open space. The cool, clean air felt awesome. I watched Dan free fall all the way down to two thousand feet and pop his parachute.

When we landed, all the skydivers ran over to congratulate me. It wasn't like I'd accomplished anything special, but I felt no fear. I didn't have anything to prove and I had everything to be thankful for.

We arrived back at the hospital thirty seconds before eight o'clock, and I told my roommates everything that had happened. They all concluded that I was crazy to get back in an airplane, but they loved the fact that I was able to. When you can celebrate somebody else's victories with joy even when you don't have your own, that is selfless love.

The momentum of my recovery kept accelerating, yet my

roommates were pretty much the same. They were all facing a very long haul. Bob wanted to go back to law school. Roy was getting ready to go back to southern Ohio, having learned to operate his wheelchair as independently as he could at that time. Larry's neck was having a tough time, and he had anti-A respiratory problems from the tracheotomy.

My progress made me a little uneasy about the lack of theirs. Some of our conversations were very intimate, but most the time we used sarcasm to teach one another about our plight.

As I got stronger, my outings got longer. I started to get a sense from my therapist and caregivers that my time at Highland View was coming to an end. They had taken me as far as they could. Actually, the supernatural force within me had taken me further than the doctors ever dreamed.

Other people needed my bed more than I did. And I didn't want to develop an institutionalized dependency by staying too long in a place where I was routinely cared for, with food and medication provided for me. My soul was on a search that included an element of the unknown.

One warm spring day in late May, Robert and I got the idea to go visit my doctors, nurses, and caregivers at Southwest General Hospital. I got dressed in the same skinny clothes I wore to the wedding. Jim drove Robert and me to the hospital for the surprise visit.

I happened to catch Dr. Nick, the chief surgeon, while he was in consultation with a visiting plastic surgeon. When he saw me, he jumped out of his chair with a happy but shocked look on his face and shouted, "Oh, my God, it's you! Look at you! I can't believe it. I just can't believe it!" He introduced me to the plastic surgeon and then rattled off a list of my complications. The various kinds of burns—first, second, and third degree…fatal. Head trauma…fatal. The chronic infections…fatal. Sepsis in my blood and tissue surrounding my organs…fatal. He must have mentioned at least six things with fancy medical terminology, and he really enjoyed saying the word *fatal*.

Not only was I alive, I was not in a wheelchair, I had no leg braces. I stood eye to eye with a man who'd said there was no way I was coming out of the woods. He couldn't have been happier that he was wrong.

He told me to go surprise the physical therapist, who was equally as shocked and just as happy to see my miraculous improvements.

As I walked past the first-floor nurse's station, the head nurse was coming out from behind the desk. She had just fixed a tray of medication, divided into individual paper cups for all the patients. When she got her first look at me, she turned as white as her uniform and dropped the tray. As pills scattered all over the floor, she whispered, "I never thought you could live." She looked like she'd just seen a ghost, but I was the opposite of a ghost.

"Yeah, I've come a long way, but I've got quite a ways to go," I said, wanting to put her at ease. "I'm still at Highland View. It's quite a place."

When we drove out of there, I had a good feeling about a bad memory in my life. My declaration to walk out of that hospital, which I never did, got fulfilled by my walking back into the place where I came and left by ambulance.

(Years later I found out about other incredible stories that took place in the lives of people who saw me and cared for me at my worst.)

Part of the healing process was to get off certain medications, including pain pills. While I still had pain, I was going to have to stiffen up and live with it. No more sleeping meds. I did have to take over-the-counter antacids to guard against acid in my stomach. The hole in my belly had shrunken from about a quarter inch to a very small opening. The doctors assured me it would continue to close up. It had already closed inside my stomach wall, and the rest of the muscles in the outer layers would close by themselves. So I wore a four-by-four-inch gauze bandage heavily taped over the little opening.

As the weeks went by, I pushed myself even harder in physical therapy. I got my right arm to raise two thirds of the way up to the top. That was a far cry from where I started.

The primary care surgeon put me in touch with the prominent plastic surgeon from Case Western University Hospital in Cleveland. He examined me and told me that the next phase would be reconstructive surgery. The plan was to give me a little time off at home to prepare for this.

My therapists and caregivers gave me paperwork and instructions for my next steps. They all shook their heads in disbelief seeing the miraculous transformation that had occurred in the previous 160 days.

God once told the scattered people of Israel, "Instead of bronze I will bring gold."[15] I'd asked God for a second chance. I gave Him ashes, and He was giving me gold.

Seventeen

Walking the Line

"We're gonna miss you," Larry said as I emptied my bedside table into a small box. It was June 28, 1969, and I was being discharged from Highland View. Although dozens of surgical procedures still lay ahead for me, it was no longer necessary for me to be an inpatient.

The long-awaited day had finally come, and I was going home! "So, what are you planning to do out there, now that you're a free bird?" asked my friend Bob.

"I don't know," I answered. "I'll just have to figure it out. But I do know I'm going skydiving again."

"You really did have a bad head injury," Larry joked.

I knew both of these men were going to require a lot more time in this hospital because they were both quadriplegics. Their futures were uncertain. But they weren't jealous. They were genuinely happy that one of us was breaking out.

These men were my loving comrades. We all had seemingly hopelessly challenges, yet we'd found life in bearing one another's burdens. An appropriate song about our relationship would be "He Ain't Heavy, He's My Brother." Yet we stuck to small talk, because saying good-bye would have taken us to a place we didn't want to go.

"I never thought you'd be leaving here," admitted a nurse's aide who was helping me to get my stuff together. "I wouldn't have given two cents for you when they rolled you in here last January." She said she had never witnessed anything as amazing as the miracles that took place.

"Yeah, he was a real mess," said Bob. "But now look at him. This kid could make a huge fortune selling fire insurance." We all joked around until it was time for me to leave. Then I stood to my feet and headed for the door. As far as I was concerned, I was walking out of that room and ending a season in my life. I would no longer be called a hospital patient or a burn victim. I was mentally and emotionally done with sickness and the daily medical routines. When I went out the front door of the hospital and the summer sun hit me, I was a free man.

When I arrived home, I wanted to call all my friends and say, "Hey, everybody, I'm out." But college, marriage, and Vietnam had scattered many of my classmates and friends. And those who were still in the area had changed. My formerly familiar hometown had become a bizarre world of bell-bottoms, earth shoes, long hair, and love beads. I didn't know how I was supposed to dress or how I should behave. I felt like Rip Van Winkle. I'd only been out of circulation for about a year, but everything seemed different.

I felt like Dorothy having returned to Oz. "This is my own house, my own room. Mom, you're here, and Robert and Jimmy, you're here. We're all together. There's no place like home."

I'd never seen my mother so happy in her entire life. They were plenty of smiles, and whatever food I could eat magically appeared by her loving hands. My mother possessed heroic strength to go through what she did—getting divorced, losing her house, and suddenly seeing me go through a complete disaster. To persevere under pressure doesn't just build character, it reveals it. Part of the word *persevere* is *severe*. But now there was a lifting of the severity.

About a week later, three buddies from my football team stopped by our house for a visit. Clint was the only one of those three who saw me while I was in the hospital, and he seemed impressed by the progress I'd made. "You're looking…better, Mickey. Really."

Bob hadn't seen me since before the accident. He stared at me so much, I could tell he was nervous. "Wow, man, what happened?" Obviously he knew what happened, but seeing me like that was shocking.

Trying to break the tension in the room, I joked, "I may look weird, but how many people do you know with a paisley complexion?" My scarred skin was multicolored from the silver nitrate I was treated with. And paisley was in style in 1969.

We exchanged memories of our football days and some of our high school pranks. The guys didn't stay very long. It was great to see them even if just to reminisce.

In all fairness, I did look a lot different. The people who saw me at my worst would say I was much better. But to anybody who knew me before or saw me in public, I was a shockingly disfigured individual who would unnerve anybody.

My right eye looked like a blue-gray giant cataract that was still partly sewn shut. Half of my face and the whole side of my head and neck were horribly tight, discolored, and scarred.

When you meet someone, the person's face is the first thing you see. And mine was a mess. My once shiny mane of hair ended about three inches above where my right ear used to be. My right arm and hand appeared relatively useless, with all of the fingers amputated and something resembling a pointy thumb. I was probably the cause of more than a few car accidents because people were rubbernecking. They couldn't take their eyes off me if they saw me on a sidewalk. But compared to what I was at my worst, my situation was miraculous.

As my three buddies left, all going in different directions than I was, I wondered, *Where do I belong?* This question is common to all humankind. In the search for significance, the heart asks, *Who am I? What am I supposed to do?* I had survived certain death, and I climbed a huge mountain by recovering my ability to walk. But where was I walking to?

A few days after their visit, Dan Harding parked his car in front of our house. My brother went to the screen door and saw him standing outside the trunk of his car.

"Hey, Robert," Dan called out, "tell your brother to close his eyes. I've got something to show him that's going to blow his mind."

I closed my eyes, and I heard Dan march right to me. "Okay, you can look now." When I opened my eyes, I saw a brand-new Super-Pro parachute harness and container, state-of-the-art and as light as a feather. "Your red, white, and blue Para-Commander is packed inside it."

"Wow!" I'd seen a picture of this in the latest *Parachutists* magazine. But I didn't know anybody had one yet.

"Think you'll be ready to go three weeks from Saturday?"

He had thrown down a challenging gauntlet, and I assured him I was eager to accept.

"It'll just be me, you, and Robbie. And we're gonna keep it a secret. We won't tell anybody until the time comes." As I gazed at that parachute, a longing to go skydiving again infused me—not only because I'd had so much success with it before the accident, but also because that small group of elite skydivers had stuck with me through the tough times. That's out of character for this group of people. They all lead busy lives, and this passion requires tremendous time and resources.

On one of my last days in the first hospital before going to rehab, the owner of the skydiving club came to see me along with another skydiver. They set up a projector in my room and played a 16 mm film of the latest air-to-air skydiving expertise, produced by the most prestigious man who made these movies. It was very inspiring. But even more important to me was the generous spirit of these men to put everything together and then drive two hours to give me a boost when I really needed it.

As I prepared for my first jump since the accident, I mentally reflected on this activity that had been second nature to me. It didn't occur to me to be afraid or to get into any kind of special shape. But I did wonder, being sixty pounds lighter than before, if I weighed enough to fall all the way to the earth without being captured by the jet stream. I imagined the six o'clock news report: "There's a cold front coming in tonight. And wow, is that guy still circling the earth after his jump last week?"

Dan called Thursday evening. "Change of plans. We're going a week early. I checked the weather and it's going to be perfect Friday, Saturday, and Sunday. You ready to go?"

"I was born ready."

At 6:30 Saturday morning Dan arrived to pick me up, along with Robert and my mom. We hadn't told her we were going to skydive. She thought we were just going out for a picnic. When we arrived at the Cleveland School Sport of Parachuting Club, she figured out something was going on. "Hey," she said, "what are you boys doing?"

"It's okay, Sparrow," Dan said, using his favorite nickname for my mom, chosen because she was so little and his nickname was the Eagle. "I'll take good care of him. Just watch the target area."

We watched the airplane go up a few times and drop other skydivers, who all landed perfectly. At high noon, I put on my jumpsuit, boots, and that beautiful new parachute rig. Then Dan, Robert, and I got in the plane. Dale, the pilot and owner of the club, put a special pad on the floor for my comfort, and we were up, up, and away. We were going to the top floor—12,500 feet.

The closer that small aircraft got to jumping altitude, the more peaceful I felt. I stood on the step, Robbie perch on the edge, and all of us went out together as quickly as we could. My light weight caused me to fall slower, but in about ten seconds, after falling a thousand feet, we formed a perfect star. I held my leg up to create a rudder, and we spun around in circles like a propeller. When I put up the other leg, we went the opposite direction. For sixty seconds, I felt like I was suspended indefinitely in pure, rare air.

At 2,500 feet we turned in opposite directions and tracked away from each other. I had a beautiful opening. Robbie and Dan opened slightly lower. Because and I was so thin and a light, I stayed aloft a lot longer. What a spectacular view! And the silence was so tranquil.

My landing was spot on—with hardly any impact. As I stood still while the parachute floated to the ground, the national champion and the best skydivers on the planet ran up to congratulate me. And they all signed my logbook! I looked into their grinning faces, very appreciative of their celebration. But unlike every jump I'd made before, I didn't feel anxious to keep doing it. Something else was attracting me, though I wasn't sure what it was.

A week later, I had to go back to Highland View because the small hole in my stomach was not closing as expected. The surgeon made a vertical incision about five inches long through my stomach wall, sliced through the fat tissue (what little there was), then cut all the muscles in half. After that, all the layers of my skin were sutured tightly to make sure there was a good closure.

No one told me how much this would hurt! Every move of my diaphragm was excruciating. If I coughed, burped, or turned the wrong way, the pain was unbelievable. The nurses gave me morphine, but I was so used to it, I needed a horse's dose just to take the edge off.

After the procedure, I wrapped a large towel around myself and pulled it tight to keep the muscles from expanding against the stitches. After a few days, Robert found it entertaining to make me laugh. When I did, I had to pull that towel tightly around me, like a woman putting on a nineteenth-century corset.

When the incision healed, I looked like I had two belly buttons. Doctors told me I couldn't do anything strenuous for several months. Of course that meant skydiving was out. What would I do for excitement?

I didn't have a car of my own, so my daily routine was full of empty space. I stayed in contact with Dan Harding, mostly on the phone because he was so busy skydiving. I also stayed in touch with some of the other skydivers with whom I had developed a special bond. But they were also busy making jumps at the club.

So I listened to music. A lot. I explored the psychedelic experience, which included expanding the mind with various drugs that supposedly enabled users to attain a mystical and spiritual understanding of life. When the Beatles went to India on a journey of Eastern religions, they became strong endorsers for transcendental meditation. Other "truth seekers" held training sessions in rented places, even churches. The promise of TM was that you could have "inner peace."

In the pop/psychedelic music, there was also a lot of talk about love. Previously all of the love songs were about boyfriends and girlfriends, sometimes husbands and wives. This music spoke of a new kind of love—love everybody, free love, love nature, and love whoever you're with. The *concept* of love was raised above a *relationship* in love.

Radical is the most accurate term I could use to describe the changes in the people around me. Long hair with beards and mustaches were common, along with tie-dyed or flannel shirts, sandals in the summer, and work boots when the weather cooled off. The girls wore bell-bottoms or long, flowing skirts. Bras were optional, and modesty was for the old-fashioned. Moral boundaries were in a state of flux. Peace and freedom included the acceptance, and even the celebration, of things that were formerly considered out of bounds. Engaging in these activities made you seem like a pioneer to some people, while others viewed you as a degenerate.

The boundary lines were not just moved; there were eliminated. The need for ultra-secretive pot smoking in the woods or in some empty building was over. Though it was still illegal, everyone talked about it freely. Many people were turned-on potheads and proud of it.

I got a close look at how music was made by going to a rehearsal of an emerging band. These singers and musicians had extreme talent, and they were putting together music that covered some of most popular classic rock bands of that time. They were able to pull off Hendrix and Clapton, as well as rearrange classic blues into highly amplified blues/rock.

The rehearsal was in an old wooden building. The high ceiling and everything inside was black. Cables ran everywhere, connected to big amplifiers that made the music really loud. In between songs they took breaks that involved a lot of marijuana smoking and discussion about the music and the sound. After being there for a while, I felt obligated to stay, even though I felt uncomfortable.

I didn't participate in the pot smoking. One of the other patients at Highland View had offered me a cigarette, but when I lit up, it was like I was smoking for the first time. My body knew that sucking hot smoke into my lungs was bad, so it tried to help me out by coughing like Doc Holliday. After that, I had no desire to smoke any kind of cigarette.

One day, some of my old friends I used to smoke grass with

came over to see me and invited me to go for a ride. After parking their VW bus in a secluded place in the Metropark, they offered me the latest and greatest wonder weed. I naïvely accepted, believing they wanted to be cool with me.

Whether I was no longer used to it or the stuff was a lot stronger, I got really high. In the days ahead, I was introduced to a group of people who smoked marijuana daily and also using psychedelic drugs like LSD.

As a result of my spiritual encounters, I had a natural tendency to love everybody and not find fault with anything. The ideology of the music fit like eclectic pieces into a puzzle I was trying to put together to figure out what my life was all about. Love and peace were very real to me, so I found it easy to identify with the peace movement.

For some reason, people kept giving me high-powered marijuana for free. It was enjoyable in some ways. The music sounded better, food tasted better, everything was funny, and time went by very slowly. But time didn't matter to me. I didn't have a job or bills to pay, and I didn't have a steady girl.

I'd never been into alcohol, but I was seriously addicted to the strongest medical drugs, such as morphine, Demerol, barbiturates, and other tranquilizers. In the hospital, I went through cold-turkey withdrawal more than once. With marijuana, the high was very comforting, and doing it with small groups gave me a sense of being with underground comrades.

I got invited to an overnight party with some of Danny's new friends. The parents were building a huge house about an hour away in the country. Their kids, who were my age, were using the secluded guesthouse for an all-out psychedelic party.

As the sun was going down, out came the party favors. These people were sophisticated users of very strong marijuana.

Someone asked me if I'd ever had "blotters." I had no idea

what a blotter was, but I said no, trying to play it cool. The guy laid out several dozen one-inch squares of paper with an off-color dot in the middle.

"This is the purest form of acid in the world," said the party host. "Just put it on your tongue and let it dissolve."

I did as he instructed. So did a couple of other guests. The music got louder and stronger. But after forty-five minutes, I hadn't noticed any other effect from the LSD.

"Take another one," said the host with a sneering I-dare-you look on his face.

I decided to wait a little longer. A few minutes later, the first dose started to kick in. It was a mind-altering, extrasensory experience. The inside of the house started breathing with me. The shadows of the people on the walls danced to the music. I didn't see anything that wasn't there, but the visual effect was like looking through a kaleidoscope into a fun-house mirror.

After the initial captivating euphoria, everything tilted. Mentally and emotionally it went from being surrealistic, to paranoia-inducing, and then terrifying.

After a few hours of trying to make it go away, I went outside into the starlit night and tried to compose myself. *Have I taken poison?* I recalled a recent news report: "June 22, 1969, Judy Garland dies of a drug overdose." I was so afraid, I stuck my finger down my throat and made myself throw up. After a few hours, the effect started to wind down. I thanked God it was ending.

As the sun began to rise, some of the young men invited me to go to a music festival. They showed me the lineup of rock stars; it was quite impressive. Still somewhat disoriented from this awful experience, I got into the car with them. Before they got out of the driveway, I had a sudden moment of rational thinking and common sense. "Stop," I said. "I can't go. Please let me out."

I later discovered they were going to Woodstock. The dates of

Woodstock, August 15–18, 1969, were the one-year anniversary of my airplane crash. That would've been a disaster for me.

Some of the language we use today was derived from the drug culture, like "What a bummer" or "That's a bad trip." Those two statements reflect how bad taking a risk with your mind and emotions can be. But in the worst of it, I cried out to God, and He threw me a lifeline.

After I got home, I reflected with a sober mind. How could this insanity help to launch a peace movement?

There is a thief who comes to steal, kill, and destroy. But there is one stronger than the thief, and He gives life and gives it in abundance.[16] This Person is not to be taken for granted.

Eighteen

In Pursuit of Peace

Down the road from our house was a small park with several walking trails where I could get quiet and think. In the hospitals I had relied completely on others for care and direction. Now I had to figure out my future. My walks provided tranquility, where I didn't have to try to figure everything out. Direction would occur by just coming into the quiet.

Peace was a big deal in that era. The circle with the peace symbol inside it was a more prolific brand than Coca-Cola. The two-fingered peace sign was the salute of that generation. Those who were of a different mind-set either looked straight ahead or gave the one-finger I-don't-like-you salute. The appropriate response to that was just a bigger smile.

I scraped enough money together to buy a car, then ventured out. Kent State University was about an hour's drive from where I lived, and there were several streets there that had club after club of young people listening to music. It wasn't about dancing or looking for somebody to meet; it was about hearing "new sounds" in the meaning of the message.

I was particularly interested in one band that had an electric guitar, a bass guitar, and drums. The audience eagerly anticipated hearing the songs they knew, yet also longed for the element of surprise. I didn't always know what the songs meant to those who wrote them, but the lyrics often they spoke to me. I developed a passion for peace and universal love, and I wanted to change the world.

After Labor Day in 1969, I received my first reconstructive plastic surgery at University Hospital in Cleveland, Ohio. This was a prestigious teaching hospital and I was a classic object lesson. I never wore hospital clothes, which helped my disposition.

Dr. John was my doctor for the next five and a half years, conducting and overseeing more operations that I could count. The first was a scar-tissue release on the right side of my face, with an L-shaped, full-thickness graft off of the left side of my neck. It was a spectacular success. But it really hurt.

The physical pain was secondary compared to the agony of waiting to see if the procedure had actually worked. Was there enough blood supply from the right side of my face to support that large of a piece of tissue?

Fortunately, when the stitches came out, the graft looked perfect. As a matter of fact, the procedure went so well, Dr. John performed another one. Right down the middle of my nose was severe scar tissue, and I had no nostril on the right. The plan was to cut off about a third of my left ear skin and cartilage, then turn it upside down to make a nose.

After this procedure, the operating team and a lineup of medical students came into my room to see how it came out. They were all smiles. Someone handed me a mirror, and I was amazed. I had a new nose!

Seven days later they removed the stitches and all of the gauze packing inside my nose. But when they pulled out the packing, the bottom part of my nose came off with it. They made a little adjustment to what was left from the first operation and fashioned me another nose as best they could.

The doctors were really disappointed, and so was I. But I figured, *You win some and you lose some.* My goal was to heal.

I had a private room and the nurses were very nice to me. I got to know them all by name and even learned a little bit about their lives.

When alone in my room, I listened to the radio. I had some visitors, but this time I wasn't in danger. I recovered from these surgeries faster and better than the initial ones. My only concern was that my doctor seemed reluctant about giving me a lot of detail about the procedures.

I heard on the radio that there was going to be a large war moratorium at Kent State in mid-October, with national speakers and live music. I connived my doctor into letting me out early so I could attend, promising to take good care of myself. As I left with a suitcase full of bandages, he gave me my instructions. Then he grinned. "I want you back here in about two and a half weeks." I promised to return.

It was good to get home. The suture lines on my face were healing very well. The additional tissue relieved a great deal of the tightness on my face and neck. I was eating pretty normally and steadily gaining weight.

My favorite band, the James Gang, was playing a couple of nights before the moratorium, so I drove to Kent early to hear them. The whole town was abuzz about the upcoming event.

The band was exceptional, and though the place was packed, I got a place right in front of the stage. No one talked about the moratorium. It seemed to be understood that everybody was going to be there to make a stand against the war.

The day before the event, I went to a craft store and got various colors of Day-Glo paint. I decorated my blue Chevy Impala with flowers and colorful designs. I wrote "Peace" on the front and back, and "Get It Together" on both sides of the car.

When I stopped at a tollbooth on the Ohio Turnpike, the uniformed man gave me a funny look as he gawked at my car. "Get *what* together?" he asked.

I smiled and said, "Peace."

He shook his head and waved me through.

On the day of the event, all of the local businesses were closed. The march took place in an open outdoor area with a large platform for the speakers and the band. In addition to many young people from college, there were business people and families. Men, women, and children all wore black armbands and walked silently to the open grounds.

This wasn't just a war moratorium. It was a passionate "teach-in," with facts and figures presented by the speakers, punctuated by applause and spontaneous standing ovations. The crowd was huge, but orderly. Everyone was sober, yet peaceful.

As the music escalated, someone grabbed my left hand and said, "Come with me." I recognized her. She was the wife of the lead guitarist. She led me onto the stage with a lot of other people singing "Give Peace a Chance," the John Lennon anthem for the peace movement. For about ten minutes, which seemed like forever, the same words were repeated over and over, in unison and with strong feeling. That sea of people, with one mind and one voice, stood in agreement for the same thing: an end to the war and to violence in general. Weaving back and forth, united hand-in-hand, they made a human chain.

As I drove home on the turnpike, I felt a great sense of belonging. At that moment, I truly believed we could change the world.

Early the next morning I drove to a large park for a long walk, meditating on the concept of peace. I'd heard quite a bit of the Eastern religious versions of "inner peace," but this was a call for political and social peace. In the quiet of that walk in the woods, I felt both inner peace and peace all around me. There wasn't any music or people making passionate speeches. The peace I experienced was bigger and deeper than even the beauty of nature.

I looked at my right hand. *A year ago there was no hope for me and I was dying.* The fiery autumn leaves framed by the deep blue sky was a vivid reminder that life has seasons. I was learning how to see, hear, interpret, and respond. I wanted to heal the violence that was in the world, but I was still very much in the midst of a season of healing myself.

The following Monday I checked back into University Hospital and met with Dr. John and two others on his team. He described the next step: a bold attempt to restore my right hand to useful function. The doctors were so confident and matter-of-fact, the procedure sounded routine. But I knew that doctors always spoke to patients with a positive attitude.

The next day I did preoperative testing, met with the anesthesiologist, and got a chest X-ray and blood work. The usual process. I'd become really good at getting revved up to have a big operation. It was like getting pumped up for a playoff game.

But this procedure was going be long and involved. My hand was fused with scar tissue and some tendons had stuck together.

The first step of reconstruction was to remove the tight scar tissue. The surgeon stripped all the scar tissue from what was left of my right hand, like peeling off a glove. The exposed tissue was completely raw down to the muscle and blood vessels. Next he hollowed out a pouch of skin in the area between my chest and my belly button. He lined it with a large split-thickness graft taken from my buttock. My hand was inserted into the opening of a horizontal kangaroo pouch, which was sewn up across my wrist and then pulled tightly all around my right hand.

This complex procedure took all day, resulting in extensive blood loss and intense pain. The open space of my bent elbow was packed and taped with enough gauze and wadding to immobilize my arm for the next six weeks. This was done to allow enough time for my body to grow new blood vessels from my right arm into the skin graft and the fat tissue that was going to grow on and around my right hand. During that time, I think I broke the record for the longest continuous imitation of Napoleon in history.

After six weeks Dr. John and his team began the first step of the removal process. Dr. John wanted to make sure there was enough blood coming from my right arm into the newly grafted tissue around my hand. So after injecting me with several large doses of Xylocaine to numb the nerves, he made the incision—with me wide awake and watching! Blood ran down my side as he stitched the outer edges around my hand.

Two days later, the doctor checked my hand and decided I was a go for total removal. This time they put me to sleep, because there was going to be lots of work to close the tissue around my hand and the large area on my chest.

When Dr. John and his young disciples came into my room after the procedure, they were all smiles. It felt good to have my hand released after being stuck against my chest for six weeks! There was significant pain involved, but I was happy for the good report.

Five days later, as the doctor unraveled the bandage from my wrist down, I got my first look at my hand. It looked like I had a little boxing glove on my formerly useless hand, but it was a pretty pink color.

Two days later, in the middle of the afternoon, the head nurse came in with a young male resident. I identified the syringe on her tray as being full of morphine. *Why am I getting this shot in the middle of the day? I didn't ask for any painkillers.* The nurse administered the morphine and said they'd come back in twenty minutes after it took effect.

The young resident returned and told me to take off my shirt. He unwrapped the top of the bandage on my chest and gave it a quick tug, pulling it off. When the air hit the donor site on my chest, the pain was extraordinary. The young doctor apologized. Then I heard him mumble, "Why do they give us guys these kind of jobs to do?"

After several days, I talked to Dr. John about going home. He first said no, but I promised him I wouldn't do anything except sit around and heal. I agreed to take with me all the dressings and medication to guard against infection. This was serious, but he trusted my experience with bandages and my knowledge of healing.

Since there was going to be a couple weeks of recuperation at home before we could go on to the next step, I bought an acoustic guitar and taped a large pick on the end of the bandage of my right hand. I had not picked up a guitar since the sixth grade, and I wasn't very good at it then. This time, I sat for hours learning chords and making up progressions. I didn't just hear the music; I felt it. I learned a couple of folk/rock songs, but I found the most enjoyment playing along with the music on my stereo LP records.

I changed my dressings every day. My hand looked really good, but the site on my chest was healing a little more slowly. Thankfully, it didn't hurt as much as when that young doctor ripped the bandage off.

I was getting the hang of playing the guitar. I couldn't do any finger picking because I didn't have any fingers! But I could play the chords rhythmically and I picked up some bass and lead lines.

After a few days, I determined my surgical wounds were healed enough for me to sneak off to Kent State University and go to JB's to hear the James Gang again. I got there early and saw the front door had a note scribbled on it, saying. "Tonight: Glass Harp." *Who the heck is Glass Harp?* I went in anyway and nestled into a booth on the left side of the stage.

Glass Harp was a three-piece band like the James Gang, with

a big drum set, a bass guitarist, and an electric guitarist. They played a medley of familiar songs from the Beatles to Jimi Hendrix, along with classic blues-rock. I was blown away! They played some of the clearest music I'd ever heard, with incredibly crisp melodic vocals. The lead guitarist, Phil Keaggy, who was also the lead singer, was amazing. He was maybe eighteen or nineteen years old, and without a doubt the best guitar player I had heard either in person or on any record.

From that night on I didn't want to miss any opportunity to hear Glass Harp and this brilliant young guitarist Phil Keaggy.

When I returned to the hospital, my plastic surgeon asked with a grin, "Are you ever going to cut your hair?"

I didn't think he really cared how long my hair was. He was just pleased at how well the surgeries were going.

"Let me show you something." He opened a petri dish that had a clear substance in it. "This is a silicon ear resembling the cartilage that was your right ear."

"Wow. How does that become my ear?"

"I make a curved incision right behind where your right ear was, put a skin graft underneath, and suture the silicon to your skull. The skin will grow through it." The silicon prosthetic had little mesh-like holes in it, and my skin would grow through it and become a real ear. There was nothing wrong with the hearing mechanism in my ear; there just wasn't anything left of the original ear except part of my lobe, which would get incorporated in the surgery.

The next morning, I was in the operating room before seven. A nurse gave me the pre-op shot, which put everybody to sleep except me. As the attendant rolled me in, I heard one of the young doctors joking with the nurse, "Did you get all hot and bothered about this young man and chew his ear off?" I started laughing, and they all got embarrassed.

Medical professionals sometimes joke around in surgery, especially if they think the patient can't hear them. But the personnel at University Hospital always treated me with respect and honor. They tried to make my stay there as enjoyable as possible. But I was a challenge to their skills, like a block of beautiful marble to Michelangelo.

In the recovery room, I woke up with my head bandaged, looking like the soldiers in the painting *The Spirit of '76*. After returning to my room, I took off my hospital gown and put on my cutoffs and a colorful T-shirt. I had my guitar in the hospital with me, so I taped a large guitar pick on my still-bandaged hand, closed the door quietly, and played the blues—but they were happy blues. After several minutes two young nurses came in and said, "Hey, that's really cool." My head hurt, and so did the spot where they took the skin graft from, but the more I played, the less I felt it. Music can be a therapeutic part of healing.

Six days later my doctor and all of his disciples filled my room. A drum roll would have been in order as they unwrapped the bandage. A round of applause broke out as they looked at a perfectly pink reconstructed ear where there had been none. It was a victory for me and the entire surgical team.

The doctor was worried about infection because a foreign material, silicon, had been implanted in my tissue with grafted skin. So he kept me in the hospital a lot longer. That gave me a chance to play my guitar more.

I was scheduled to get out right before Christmas. The previous Christmas I was barely alive, and in the natural I didn't have much hope. This Christmas I was going home walking, playing the guitar, and listening with a new ear. I also went home with a song in my heart, deep down in my spiritual being: "Peace on Earth and goodwill to all mankind."

One of the first things I wanted to do after I got home was to visit my friend Dr. William Jeric. I wanted to show off his medical colleagues' handiwork. We zoomed through all the cool stuff that had been surgically done, and then he wanted to show me some of his work. I watched hundreds of slides of medical operations that he'd performed on civilians for thirteen months in Vietnam. He worked twelve hours a day, seven days a week, bringing some relief to the horrors created by modern warfare. While showing me the pictures, he often stopped to explain the severity of some of the surgeries. In the United States, death or failure could have resulted in a malpractice suit. But there he wasn't paid a penny. It was a mission of mercy...and a very successful one.

In the middle of our conversation, Bill told me, "I hate organized religion, but the only explanation for what happened to you is the miraculous grace of God."

I shared with him some of my spirit experiences, then talked about physical therapy and the medical stuff—things I thought he'd be interested in. He gently put his hand on my forearm and said quietly, with tears in his eyes, "Mickey, you are beautiful."

"Thank you," I said, holding back tears. Anytime God is recognized, God is glorified.

Shortly after New Year's Day, my skydiving buddy Jerry invited me to go to central Florida to attend a parachuting competition. He had just gotten a brand-new Jaguar XKE convertible. We drove in shifts—mine was crossing the Georgia/Florida state line.

The sun was rising and the eight-track tape player was playing the Beatles' "Here Comes the Sun." I couldn't see anybody in front of me or behind me, so at 145 miles per hour we blew into Florida. I had never driven a car that fast, and I'd never been in one that could safely do that.

We got to Kissimmee and put on our parachutes. As we were getting ready to board the plane for our first jump, the owner of the club said, "You were in that Cherokee that went down in

Ohio." Serious skydivers make up a very small circle of people, so everybody knew about my accident. He seemed honored that I was jumping at his facility.

We made a few jumps over a couple days, then went to the competition. I socialized with the men and women who were preparing for the World Cup skydiving meet. But I didn't compete myself. My skydiving skills were okay considering how I was physically because of the surgery and rehabilitation. However, skydiving didn't have the same allure it used to have.

When we got back to Cleveland, I went back to University Hospital. When Dr. John examined my ear, he was shocked that it was so healed. He told me there were far more failures than successes with that type of transplant.

The next step would be a radical configuring through surgery of my right hand, which was enclosed in fat, smooth-as-a-baby's-behind glove of grafted tissue. It would take place as soon as possible.

I got invited to a party in Toronto, Canada, with some of the skydivers from our club in Ohio. I knew some of the Canadian team members because they occasionally came down to practice at our club. We all went out to a nice spot to hear a live blues band our host was recording on a reel-to-reel tape machine. Then we all ventured back to his pad to listen to the recorded music. The party was going to continue on into the night, and two of the guys from Ohio invited me to go to the university section in the heart of the city.

We wound up in a trendy coffeehouse with black lights and pictures of San Francisco. The patrons were freely smoking marijuana and hashish, a high-grade derivative. One of the guys with me was going to stay in the coffeehouse and keep partying, so another guy and I decided to walk back to our hotel room less than a mile away. The night air was perfectly still, and snowflakes as big as silver dollars floated from the dark sky.

A man stood on our walkway with his back toward me. Large snowflakes dotted his long, dark hair. When I was about two feet away, he turned and looked at me. His eyes penetrated deep into my soul. His face reflected a sad countenance.

I knew it was Jesus. His presence supernaturally altered the atmosphere so that the sights and sounds totally changed. When my companion began talking, each syllable echoed a thousand times in two seconds. I felt like I was in a giant reverberation chamber.

As we walked past Jesus, I tried to say something to my companion. Words vibrated out of me as if there was a spiritual bubble surrounding us. I was in spiritual shock.

I sensed that the Lord wasn't condemning me; rather, He had an all-knowing compassion for me. He knew everything about me, and His flood of strong love and compassion was undeniable. I was overwhelmed. I stopped trying to talk.

As I walked back speechless to the hotel room, the image of Jesus' face was continuously on my mind's viewing screen. I pondered, *Why the sad countenance?* As I tried to reason it out, my thoughts ricocheted between right and wrong, good and evil, earthly and natural as well as spiritual. I was saturated with wonder about His feelings for me.

My friends were unaware of what was happening to me. When they awoke the next morning and began to talk, I became increasingly uneasy. They seemed superficial, cynical, and sarcastic—almost mockingly evil.

I'd traveled to Toronto expecting to have some fun with friends between severe operations. Now I couldn't wait to get away from them and get back home to Cleveland.

Still spiritually stunned, I was unable to talk for thirty-six hours. I had never felt so alone.

When the spiritual shock wore off, I needed to find peace,

but I couldn't go for one of my walks in the park because it was too cold. I decided to go to my room and listen to records on the stereo. What normally would have entertained me now seemed flat and repetitious.

That weekend, I decided to go to Kent State and listen to some live music. I got to JB's early, as the warm-up band was setting up. I found a seat on the right side of the stage.

Glass Harp came out of the gate like a rocket. John, the drummer, was soaking wet with sweat after the first song, like usual.

But there was something different about Phil Keaggy. His guitar licks were hotter than ever. But it was like I could see light beaming from his face. He wasn't just singing words; he was releasing something that was being carried within the words.

As he introduced some new songs, I noticed he was wearing a rawhide necklace with a large wooden cross.

I'd heard Glass Harp at least ten times and thought I knew all their songs. But the next song opened with a dramatic musical intro and the words "Look in the sky." The rest of the lyrics were beautiful. I sensed that what he was singing about meant more to him than words and music.

At the end of the second set, he started talking unashamedly about Jesus. Clearly, something wonderful had happened to this young artist since I saw him last.

When the band resumed playing, I no longer just listened to the music. I was drawn into the meaning of the lyrics.

As I drove home, I smiled with amazement.

The next morning I heard some of my sister's friends say they were going to JB's that night to hear the band. I knew Glass Harp would be playing, so I decided to ride with them. I didn't tell my sister's friends what I experienced the night before.

We got good seats, as I always liked to be close. The band played, including several new songs that were about spiritual things. During the second break, Phil came over to say hi to me. "There's going to be a prayer meeting after we're done tonight," he said. "Would you like to come?"

I'd never even heard of a prayer meeting, but it seemed like a warm invitation. "Yeah. But I'll have to check with the folks I'm riding with."

I told my two companions about the opportunity. "You want us to go a prayer meeting?" They looked at me is if I were inviting them to somebody's house for knitting lessons. Clearly they weren't interested. They told me about a party they planned to go to, hosted by someone we'd gone to high school with in Independence, Ohio, who was now a student at Kent State.

Since they were my ride, I felt I had to stick with them.

As we neared our friend's house, we stopped at a traffic light. The person in the front seat rolled down her window to speak to the driver of the car stopped next to us. The driver rolled his window down and my friend said, "Hey, how would you like to come to a party? It's going be a high time."

The person's face glistened. "Yeah! As long as we can feast on Jesus." He closed his window and drove off. I felt like I was in the wrong car.

At the so-called party, which was really a gathering of about six people, a discussion about Jesus started. I found out that some of the former revolutionaries from college had become "Jesus freaks." They still looked the same, but all they talked about was the truth of the Bible, the love of God, and Jesus, who seemed like something they actually knew and who, they claimed, was coming back soon.

I didn't have much to say, but I sure was listening.

Our host declared all sorts of things about God. "I think people misunderstand religion. They talk about the end of the world, and how God is really mad at us sinners. They say He's coming back to bring fiery judgment on the earth. Well, I grew up with all this stuff in church. But what good is it? I think life is about the here and now. Karl Marx said, 'Religion is the opiate of the masses.'" Ironically, he spoke that cryptic quote while exhaling a large cloud of marijuana smoke.

I felt out of it and restless. I wished I'd gone to the prayer meeting, even though I didn't have a car.

I began to hear people talking about Jesus everywhere I went. Robert was now a junior in high school. One of his friends told us there was a group of kids his age who met in homes to play guitar, sing, and talk about the Bible. I decided to go check it out before I started my next long-term round of reconstruction surgery.

Although I was almost twenty-one in a room full of teenagers, these kids were amazingly warm, intelligent, and welcoming. I felt very comfortable as they sang folk-like contemporary Jesus songs with acoustic guitars. Steve, a man in his twenties who was the Campus Life regional leader, taught from the Bible. Since I didn't have a Bible, somebody gave me one so I could read along.

Steve might as well have been speaking Greek. He was interesting, but I hit a wall when he read, "All our righteous deeds are like a filthy garment."[17]

"What do you think that means, Mickey?" he asked.

I shrugged, perplexed.

"The best we do before God is like a pile of dirty rags."

"I don't really get that part."

"Tell me, have you ever done a good deed for someone?"

"Sure," I answered confidently.

"Because you've done good things, would you call yourself a good person? A righteous person?"

"Yeah," I answered, a lot less confidently, remembering all the times I'd made big mistakes.

Steve explained that natural man is basically self-centered, and on our own we can never make the grade of the high standard of God. He used himself as an example, sharing his personal story.

"I can't do this on my own, and neither can you," he told the group.

After a time of prayer, the meeting was over. Then Steve approached me. "I'd like to have breakfast with you tomorrow. Are you available?"

I gave him my address. He said he would pick me up.

Over breakfast we shared some small talk and got to know each other. Then we talked about my lack of understanding of what he was trying to teach the previous night. Sharing some personal examples along with passages of Scripture, he clarified the meaning to me. The best efforts of man on his own do not qualify him compared to the holiness of God. Holiness only comes through the work that Jesus finished, in what he said was called "the atonement." He went on to say that we are the righteousness of God when we're joined to Jesus.

Even though I wasn't familiar with Bible terminology, I understood what he was saying. It seemed like I already knew this deep inside. I briefly shared with him some of my spiritual encounters in the journey I had been on. I talked matter-of-factly about some things I had never told another human being.

In the middle of my personal storytelling, he burst out laughing.

"What's so funny?"

"God's got a real plan for you. You have a ministry, man."

That made less sense to me than the Bible verses I had struggled with the previous night. The only thing I knew about ministry was that it was associated with celibacy and men in black robes. I assumed he was talking about my becoming a priest, and that was too far out for me.

Over the next several days, as I prepared to enter another long haul of successive surgeries and recovery, I found comfort in playing the guitar. Just before I'd start, I would close my eyes, take a deep breath, and say, "Oh God, strengthen me." Sometimes in the middle of playing, my mind would drift off. I saw the face of Jesus looking deep into me, which brought a sense of awe and wonder.

I packed some personal items in a suitcase, grabbed my guitar, and checked in to University Hospital. My surgeon had given me the game plan in a previous visit. He was going to go in from the top of my hand, split apart some bones, and reattach some tendons that had been stuck together for more than a year and a half.

Early in the morning the anesthesiologist put me under. I woke up with a huge bandage and two stainless steel hoops sticking out of my hand like TV antennas.

I never quite got used to being anesthetized and then waking up in the recovery room, wondering, *Did they operate on me yet?* Then I felt it! *Oh yeah, they did.*

Dr. John and his faithful followers came to my room. He informed me that the procedure went far better than the original plan. The bones that had been locked up in my withered hand were moving again. But I still needed several more surgeries.

The next day I stuck my guitar pick on the bandage and tried to play. It was a bit more challenging to navigate around my guitar top and the wire hoops. And it was strange seeing metal hoops coming out of my hand going in all different directions. I played loud enough and long enough that the doctor decided to let me out early, with a load of dressings and instructions for me to play doctor.

After I'd been home two days, Robert helped me change the dressing. The skin looked healthy.

One week after the operation, I reported to the doctor's office. He took off the bandage and unscrewed the wire hoops like he was working on a ham radio. "We'll give the inside some time to finish healing, and then we'll really get it done."

A few days later I was back in the hospital. There were new X-rays, photographs, and sketches of what they were about to do in this next operation. The doctor explained that his objective was to create a functional hand with an opposing thumb. This procedure was experimental, but he seemed confident of success.

The operation took about eight hours. My surgeon and his assistant checked in on me during the late afternoon, commenting that things had gone extremely well. He also told me he was going off to medical school in the Caribbean to teach a seminar. I was to give my hand a rest…and no guitar playing.

On the third day, the associate plastic surgeon came in to change my bandage. As he unraveled the last layer of gauze, I heard him whisper, "Oh God, no."

I looked at my hand. All of the transferred skin was black, and it smelled like a dead animal. The massive operation had failed.

"I'm so sorry. We lost it all."

He said he would be back in the morning to set up a sterile field and remove the dead tissue. Then he quickly left the room.

I stared out the window and watched the sun go down. From somewhere inside me, a thought came into my mind. It was a contradiction to my logical mind, but I knew I had to follow through on it.

I rang the nurse's buzzer. When she came in, I said, "Please bring me six or seven pillows and one of those bright lights mounted on a pole."

She didn't ask me why I wanted them, probably because everyone was so upset about my situation.

I stacked up the pillows on the right side of my bed, then laid my hand and right arm on top, with the light shining on it. My scientific and biological background told me my blood vessels were clogged with hardened, coagulated blood, blocking the pathways like dried glue. And yet, I stayed up all night staring at my hand and arm, commanding blood to flow into them.

The doctor and two nurses came into my room early the next morning, adorned with gloves, masks, and gowns, to set up a sterile field around my bed. The head nurse carried a tray full of shiny, sharp instruments.

As the doctor removed my bandage, he blurted out, "I don't believe it. It's impossible." After pulling the mask off his face, he bent over the bed for a closer look. The dead tissue all around the edges of my hand was alive. There were not even red marks of inflammation. He pushed back against the wall. "I've never seen anything like this in all my years of practice." He looked afraid.

He and the nurses silently took their instruments and materials, leaving me alone. A great miracle had taken place sometime after the sun went down and before it came up again.

When Dr. John returned from the Dominican Republic, he came to see me even before he opened his mail that had been stacking up. He wanted to take the stitches out and examine my hand personally.

He stared at my stubby fingers that now worked and at my hand, which could grip. For the first time in nineteen months, I had two hands that could work together.

"Well, young man, this is not supposed to be like this. Thank God!" I'd never seen that look on his face or heard that tone of voice in his words.

Again, I received back something that was lost.

Once I got home, I enjoyed doing this using both hands that I previously had to try to do with just one. Simple things, like putting on my clothes, tying my shoes, washing my face, shaving, taking a shower.

I ran into the kitchen and grabbed a roll of tape from my

mom's utility drawer. After opening my guitar case, I grabbed a guitar pick and wrapped tape around it, twisting it so that the sticky side was on the outside. Between my newly created thumb and forefinger, I could hold a guitar pick. It felt amazing! Holding a guitar pick was like finding a treasure.

On Friday, I was off to Kent State to celebrate with a night of great music. I went by myself. I wanted to be alone. It had been many weeks since I'd been there. Spring was in the air, and spring was in me.

I was glad to see that Glass Harp was playing. The club was crowded, but I weaseled my way up to the front. It was an exceptionally good night.

During the break Phil came over and said hi. We sat on a pool table, where he showed me stuff from the Bible.

After a while he stopped and showed me his right hand. "Look, I got one too." His middle finger was a little stub.

He told me that when he was three years old, his finger got severed when he was playing with an old-fashioned well pump.

We both laughed about this odd thing we had in common.

Before he started playing again, Phil said, "There's a place I'd like you to check out." He tore off the side of a cardboard box and drew me a map with a name and a phone number on it. "It's called Grace Haven Farm. There's a bunch of people there our age who are really turned on to Jesus, and others who are really working together in community. You should go and visit."

Phil didn't know anything about my life, but there was something about him that was different from the other Jesus freaks. He was real and relatable.

On my drive home I thought about the way he showed me his hand and happily said, "I got one too." I glanced at the map he gave me and decided I needed to go there someday.

Nineteen

Peace Is a Person

A few weeks later I learned that Kent State was having some type of political rally. The fall rally had been such a positive experience for me, I decided to get up early and spend the whole day there, then enjoy an evening of music at JB's.

I parked my car and walked to the common area, where a stage and a PA system was set up. A fairly large crowd had already gathered, but nothing like it had been in the fall. Someone bellowed curses against the federal government over the loudspeaker. Just below the stage, a group of people were shouting and holding up a papier-mâché effigy of President Nixon draped with an American flag. As it was lifted higher, the rabid crowd roared with approval. The flag-draped figure was lit and suddenly exploded into flames.

I stared in disbelief. *Who are these people?* This couldn't possibly be the same crowd that sang, "Give peace a chance," last fall. These people weren't rallying for peace. This was a lynch mob, whipping themselves into a frenzy of revolutionary anger. This wasn't antiwar; this was war.

As television cameras zoomed in toward the stage and reporters frantically worked the crowd, I turned and walked away. *I can't have anything to do with this. It is not what I believe.* I believed in peace, love, and harmony.

I drove away from Kent State, too sad to stay and listen to music.

I recalled a TV interview I'd seen recently, where one of my songwriting heroes said, "Jesus Christ was the first nonviolent revolutionary." He made that statement just before playing one of his songs. Though the song was pretty and the lyrics were meaningful at the time, they no longer seemed truthful to me. Jesus was an altogether different kind of revolutionary.

Our skydiving club planned to host some of our friends from the Canadian team to prepare for the upcoming world meet. I arranged to stay with my friend, and we were going to take care of all of our guests. As usual we overdid ourselves, especially with purchasing food.

When our friends arrived with two van loads of Canadians, it was a festival. I knew most of them, but there were some new faces.

One of the guys brought a girlfriend. She seemed nice, but apparently didn't know anybody. I wanted to try to make her feel welcomed in our little circle. So I introduced myself. Then I asked, "Who are you?"

"Kathryn," she said shyly with a European accent.

I asked if she was a skydiver. She said she had been, but she'd stopped for a couple of years and was now getting back into it.

In the course of conversation I discovered she didn't have any of her own equipment. I said, "You can use my rig when I'm not using it."

She blushed. At the air field, I got on one of the first loads for thirty seconds of refreshing free fall. Later that day Kathryn used my equipment to make a ten-second free fall, which she executed very well. I made a second jump late that afternoon with some other men from our club. It was a very busy weekend, and we were all excited about the world meet, yet something felt different. I kept asking myself, *Why am I doing this? I like my friends, but I can't compete. What is wrong with me?*

The next day I was listed to go on the third load of the day along with the woman's national champion from Canada. Kathryn was using my friend's equipment on this jump. Again I had the strange feeling that something wasn't right. I shook it off and climbed in the tiny Cessna.

Kathryn was scheduled to go out first from 5,500 feet to make a free fall lasting twenty seconds—twice as long as the one the day before with my equipment. Cynthia, the Canadian champion, would go out at 6,600 feet, the prescribed altitude for style competition jumping. I was to go out last from 7,500 feet—a routine jump to work on aerial maneuvers and make a good target landing.

As Kathryn boarded the plane, I noticed that she looked a little strange. Maybe she felt intimidated jumping with the national champion on board. I flashed her a smile and give her a thumbs-up as we took off.

When we reached 5,500 feet, the pilot opened the door. Kathryn got out on the step in the classic poised position.

"Go," said the jump master.

Kathryn jumped.

We continue to climb in clockwise circles. The pilot kept looking down through his open window. When we got to 6,600 feet, it was my turn.

I had a pretty normal jump and a good shot of the target to get a dead center. But as I approached the target area, I noticed that the Canadian stylist was sitting right on the spot I was trying to hit. I pulled my steering line and made a sharp turn. After I landed, the wife of one of the men came running over to me.

"What happened?" I asked, pointing to the woman sitting on the target. "Did she get hurt?"

"Kathryn's chute never opened!"

I peeled off my harness and ran into the woods, my thoughts racing. I hoped her reserve chute had come out and she was just caught in the trees. But I was wrong. She had fallen from 5,500 feet without touching as much as a tree branch. Her small body lay facedown on the ground, like something that had never been alive.

I stood next to her and stared. She was so alive minutes ago.

A few others arrived. No one spoke. When we turned her over, I saw a small ashen hand still gripping the main ripcord.

We solemnly lifted her broken body onto the Jeep and drove slowly, keeping a distance from the crowd.

We later discovered there was nothing wrong with either of the two parachutes; she had simply frozen in fear. Two years previously, she had a total malfunction on her main parachute, but she properly opened her reserve parachute and landed safely. That's why she quit. But one of the Canada skydiving team members was her boyfriend and she wanted to be part of this group. She'd swallowed a tremendous amount of fear to do this. But not enough.

The sheriff took my information as an eyewitness. I tried to be as helpful as I could. Then I packed my gear and quietly drove off for home.

I sat in my room trying to process what had happened. I kept seeing images of Kathryn laughing and having fun, wearing my equipment one day and lying lifeless facedown the next.

Then I heard a voice whisper within me, "She just wanted to belong." This phrase repeated several times.

On May 4, 1970, five days after this tragic skydiving death, my brother ran into the house, shouting, "Did you hear what happened at Kent State? Turn on the TV."

The screen was filled with mass hysteria. The campus I knew so well had been overrun with hysterical students, ambulances, soldiers, and dozens of reporters.

The newscaster explained that the governor had ordered the

Ohio National Guard to stop the escalation of violent protests after the firebombing of the ROTC building. Earlier that day, national guardsmen had opened fire with live ammunition on a group of protesters. Four students were killed and several more seriously injured. One student who died hadn't even been part of that day's protest. She was simply walking by when a bullet struck her and killed her instantly.

The voice came to me again, saying, "It is very important what you commit your life to."

The poets and prophets of my generation were shouting about love and peace. Kathryn reached out beyond her fears because of love, and the students at Kent State stood up for peace. But now they were dead and gone. Ironically, they died seeking the very thing they thought would set them free.

I didn't know what to believe in anymore, but I knew there was something beyond all the passion and fury of my generation. There had to be.

A few days later Glass Harp was playing at a school auditorium not far from my home. I decided to go there alone.

After a few songs, in the crowded auditorium filled with young people, I closed my eyes and prayed, *Dear God, please help me. There is nobody in the whole world who knows what I'm going through, how I feel. I have no one to talk to.*

As I was thinking those words, I felt two incredibly gentle hands on my shoulders. When I opened my eyes, I saw a young girl with long brown hair and bell-bottoms standing there, tears streaming down her face. "God is so beautiful. Take Him deeper. Just keep taking Him deeper."

Small, warm waves of love washed over me—the same waves of love I felt in heaven, the same heavenly comfort I experienced when Larry spoke to me at Highland View Hospital. This love was very personal.

I heard that voice within me say, "I understand you, Mickey, and I know everything about you. I am here."

Before I could thank the young girl, she was gone. There was no way she could have known what was going on inside me. She was surely sent by God, from across a crowded auditorium, specifically to me, for that purpose. Peace came upon me that didn't need definition.

The rest of the music that night was more than music to me. It was a vertical offering, and I was part of sending it up.

As I drove home, I knew that peace was not a product of political or philosophical alignments. Nor did it come from association with a natural pleasure, like being in free fall, or a temporary non-conflict circumstance. Peace is a Person.

A few days later, I met a girl who worked at the most well-known music spot in downtown Cleveland. We had some mutual friends, and we began hanging out. Laura was about my age, very pretty, and we had some similar interests, including music. She was easy to get along with.

She was starting to get serious about our relationship when I had to go make an appointment with my doctor to discuss the next battery of surgeries..

Dr. John admitted me and explained his next operation. It was to be a radical revision of my scalp to give me a symmetrical hairline that would be landscaped around my new ear. As usual, the doctor made it sound like a good idea.

This procedure had to be done with me awake and partially sitting up. They numbed my entire head with Xylocaine. But when the shots wore off, the pain was mind-boggling! I didn't know how many nerve endings were in a human scalp, but every one of mine was screaming.

When I got out of surgery and saw the result, I was shocked. I had a reverse Mohawk.

While at home recovering, I discovered that Laura had a set of spiritual beliefs similar to many in my generation—mixing Jesus with Buddhism, mysticism, psychedelic psychology, and Native American beliefs. Kind of like spiritual minestrone soup.

One night, as we were walking arm-in-arm in the dark city, headlights from a passing car made our shadows appear together against the wall. Laura beamed. "Mickey, I think that's a sign that we will be tripping out together forever."

The more we talked about spiritual things, the more uneasy I became. I felt my inner voice say, *You cannot go on with this person.*

I told tell her we needed to break it off, at least for a while. It hurt her badly and I felt terrible.

That night, I got alone and prayed, "Dear Lord, I want the person You want for me. I don't want to hurt anybody and I don't want to get hurt. Please send me the one."

I had to force myself not to call Laura. I wanted to make her feel better, but I knew I would only make things worse.

Several weeks later, I woke up on a hot summer morning with a strong sensation. My senses were magnified with special revelation and understanding. I realized that ordinary things had deep meaning, that events on earth had an eternal connection.

This went on all day and into the evening. I tried to go to sleep, but it was impossible.

Shortly after two o'clock in the morning, three close friends pulled up outside my house. They had just returned from a three-day rock festival in Cincinnati. As I approached one of them, who was standing under the mercury-vapor streetlight, an icy chill came upon me. I knew something was terribly wrong. His face was empty, and even though he was looking right at me, his eyes were hollow. He was under the influence of some very strong drugs. I felt a strong sense of responsibility concerning this guy. I tried to talk with him, but he was in such a catatonic drug state we couldn't have a meaningful conversation.

I then realized that I was living out in real life one of the most intense scenes I saw in my vision when I was in heaven. The deep revelation I had been experiencing all day was leading me up to this, and I felt I should have done something to prevent this from happening to a close friend.

The experience was so strong and riveting, I needed someone to help me through this. After they were safely inside, I called for a cab to take me to my friend Eddie's house.

He was half-asleep as I poured out my frantic monologue about what I'd seen. I didn't want to lose the peace that was so true inside of me, yet I felt like I was trying to live in two worlds.

Suddenly, a shimmering white light about one inch in diameter outlined Eddie's neck, going around his head on both sides. "You have been given the power to be a strong influence over many people."

I knew those words were not coming from Eddie. The voice of God was speaking through my almost unconscious friend. I also knew that I had been far less than that for my severely drugged friend.

The light lifted as suddenly as it appeared. Then Eddie said, "Man, I'm really tired. Can we finish this some other time?"

Eddie wasn't even aware of what had just happened.

After he went to bed, I went into his living room, got down on my knees, and prayed. *God, I'm sorry, but I don't know what You want me to do. Show me what I'm supposed to do!*

A brilliant flash shook the windows and lit up the whole room as a bolt of lightning struck a tree in Eddie's front yard. The lightning released an immediate downpour.

I burst into tears, crying from deep inside for many minutes. When the weeping stopped, the guilt and fear I'd been feeling were washed away, and I felt waves of love rolling over me again. A cloud of peace settled upon me.

When I awoke the next morning, the sky was cloudy but the rain had stopped. The peace was still with me, yet there was also an urgency to talk to somebody about it.

I drove to St. Michael's and knocked on the rectory door. A stout man named Father Peter let me in. I gave him a mini version of my life, including being raised in that church. I couldn't talk fast enough as I told him everything, including the recent events of the skydiving tragedy and the Kent State shootings. I also shared with him my experiences with the voice of the Lord helping me. As I started to share about the previous night's events, he tried to connect a cigarette to a lighter with shaking hands.

When I got to the part about the lightning bolt at Eddie's house, lightning hit the building we were sitting in. The priest grabbed his chest and yelled, "Oh, my God!" He stood so fast, he knocked over his chair and sent his cigarette flying through the air. "I guess I'm not ready to go yet!"

The lightning strike didn't faze me; I wanted to keep talking. But the priest pushed me toward the door. He handed me a little booklet and said, "Read this."

As I took the book, I tried to speak to him again, but he cut me off.

"I don't think I can help you. Please don't come back!"

I stood alone in the hall, with a terrified priest on the other side of the door.

When I got home, I read the little catechism book he gave me all the way through. After reading the last page, I still didn't know what to do.

I began to a comparative examination of the many spiritual beliefs that were prevalent in the culture, although I did not personally experiment with any of them. Over the next two years of surgeries and rehabilitation, I found peace playing guitar and thinking about Jesus.

I lost any hope that political reform was going to change what I believed was wrong in America. My distrust and disappointment after Kent State University, and the continuation of the war in Vietnam, followed by Watergate, affected my thoughts for the future. I went from dreaming to intelligently scheming to get out of what seemed inevitable.

A new year dawned—1973—and my friend Jim wanted me to meet some girl that he knew casually through some friends we both had in Brecksville, Ohio. One cold, snowy night in February, I stood on the porch, shivering in my Italian Eskimo coat. A slender girl with long blonde hair opened the door.

"Mickey Robinson," Jim said, "meet Barbara Newport."

She seemed shy, but I was immediately drawn to her beautiful smile.

After dumping my coat where she pointed on a pile of others, I looked on her wall and saw a serene picture with the quote "Our lives are being frittered away by detail. Simplify." Thoreau was one of my favorite thinkers, so that stirred interest in me about this girl. I'd put up a relationship shield after I broke up with Laura, but as the night went on, Barbara paid attention exclusively to me, and my shield gradually lowered.

When I got home, I immediately called her on the phone and we talked until dawn. We spent day after day together, and something was awakened in me that I hadn't felt since before the accident.

We'd met the day after Valentine's Day. And I had just received an arrow through the heart.

Twenty

Man Tends, God Mends

Perhaps the phrase *Love is blind* is a reality, but during the entire evening Barbara never seemed to notice that I had any scars. She did tell me later that for her it was love at first sight. We spent every day with each other. When I went home, I called her and we talked for hours, always ending with "Good night, and have a nice dream."

Barbara was the second oldest in a family of five children. Her brother, the oldest, had been recently married. During most of her growing-up years, she bore a lot of the responsibility for the family, especially when her parents were out of town. Barbara had gone to Ohio State University, the only college her father didn't want her to attend, but dropped out over Christmas vacation because of a lack of interest.

Barbara's father was a successful senior partner in an upwardly mobile, world-class architectural firm. He had worked his way up from nothing. Born and raised in a poor Irish neighborhood in Cleveland, he was determined to be the best and was well on his way to achieving many of his goals. His plans for Barbara included marrying a doctor, a lawyer, or a super salesman like him. When he met me, I'm sure he thought I was just another one of her fad type of guys who would come and go.

The momentum of our relationship could best be compared to an avalanche, and nothing can stop an avalanche. Barbara's friends all told me, "We've never seen her like this with anybody."

Thankfully my mom really liked Barbara.

One night Barbara and her friend drove over in her dad's luxury car to pick me up to go to a dinner party in a fancy restaurant. She was wearing a black evening dress and black spike heels. She looked like a Hollywood movie star. Prior to meeting me, she had planned to go on spring break to Florida with a friend of hers, using her family station wagon.

As we discussed the seriousness of our relationship, her spring break plans changed. We drove from Florida to Jamaica and eloped! We didn't know where we were going in life. But we were really sure we were going together.

For our honeymoon, we went to an underdeveloped village in the western part of the north shore of the island of Jamaica, which had the most beautiful sugar-white sand beaches, the prettiest emerald blue water with palm trees, every tropical flower imaginable, and majestic blue-green mountains. The Jamaican locals always surrounded American visitors, because everybody from America was supposedly rich. They all wanted to be our guide. "Hey, mon, let me show you somet'ing." They offered us beads, straw hats, fresh fruit, and a strong Jamaican herb—marijuana.

I was quite a novelty to them. "Hey, crash plane man, let me come with you. I'll take good care of you, mon."

We stayed in a thatch hut right on the beach, being served breakfast every morning and dinner under the stars or by candlelight in our bamboo villa. This cost us about three dollars a night, and that included the food! I easily grew accustomed to that life.

In this romantic beach setting, Barbara and I made a simple commitment to each other. We both knew her father would never approve of our marriage, and I'd been influenced by the notion that marriage was a legally binding institution, so there could be no divorce. Also, I had some upcoming surgeries scheduled at University Hospital. Waiting for all these things to get sorted out did not serve our purposes. We decided to keep our marriage a secret until we could figure out how to tell everybody what we'd done.

After a week in Jamaica, we flew to Florida, then drove back to Ohio. We went to our separate houses and continued seeing each other without getting caught…or so we thought.

Phil Keaggy was going to be doing a concert at Barbara's old high school in her hometown of Brecksville, Ohio. Although Glass Harp had released their third studio album and were getting great recognition, Phil decided to leave the band and launch out to do acoustic music as a Christian artist.

Barbara and I went to the concert early to get good seats. As usual, the music was over the top. Phil shared about Jesus between songs. After what seemed like the last song, he gave an invitation. "There are some of you out there who need to stand up and leave everything and follow the Lord Jesus Christ."

I had never heard a challenge like that. Everything in me wanted to stand up, but I felt like weights were holding me down. What was only a moment seemed like hours. My body felt like it was on fire as time stood still. Finally, I sprang to my feet.

Phil nodded in my direction. "Thank you, brother."

I thought I was the only one standing, but when I glanced to my left, I saw Barbara standing next to me, gazing at me with total trust. We were the only two in the auditorium standing. We prayed together. Then Phil sang another song. It wasn't an encore; it was a song about thanksgiving. I felt a tremendous relief, as if those weights had been taken off of me. There's something powerful about a bold declaration.

The following Monday, I was admitted to the hospital for my

preplanned surgeries. Barbara's parents had been visiting Washington DC to look for a new house because they were planning to relocate their family. Mr. Newport was going to head up an international office for his firm. After several trips, they found a home in Potomac, Maryland, a suburb of Washington DC. Of course they expected the whole family to move together, including Barbara, beginning the month of June, only a few weeks away.

On a Wednesday, I underwent an operation to create a deepening and separating between the metacarpal bones of my first and middle finger. This was going to produce more gripping for my right hand. Skin grafts had to be applied to both sides of my finger and around the top of my hand.

Moments after I woke up back in my room, I got dressed and started walking around. The pain was excruciating, as always. I never got used to that.

The next day I cornered Dr. Thomas, an eye specialist and a famous pioneer in eye surgery. In the second year after my accident, my doctors had determined that I was not a suitable candidate for cornea transplant surgery. They felt it would be like robbing somebody else of a chance for sight to waste a donor cornea on my blind right eye. There had been too much damage scarring, so I was taken off the list.

Several times while I was at University Hospital for plastic surgery, I bugged Dr. Thomas. Finally, that day, he said, "I hear you, Mickey. Give me some time. I'll think about it."

I had a feeling there was something wrong with my hand and that someone need to change the dressing. My doctor was out of town, and the hospital's head resident was in Washington, taking his national boards to specialize in plastic surgery. So a doctor I didn't know was in charge of my case for the weekend. I called him, but he never answered.

When the hallway was empty, I snuck behind the nurse's

station and found a suture kit. The head nurse caught me taking it to my room, confiscated it, and told me it was the doctor's responsibility to change the bandage.

"I'm telling you, I can feel it needs to be changed now," I said frantically.

"You need to go back to your room. Doctor's orders."

I'd been in the hospital so many times, everybody was on a first-name basis and they gave me a lot of leeway. But this woman was a weekend nurse and she didn't really know me.

Barbara called me on the phone and told me she really wanted to come see me at the hospital, but her father wouldn't let her. I could tell she felt terrible. "I'll try to talk him into it. I really will."

But he didn't give in. I felt very vulnerable and abandoned.

My doctor came in on Monday to change my bandage. As he unwound the gauze, the skin grafts fell right off my hand onto the floor, stitches and all. The painful surgery was a total loss. He was so embarrassed he couldn't look me in the eye.

Trying to contain my grief, I went to the nurse's station and whispered, "Is there some place I can go to be alone?"

"We have a chapel on the first floor," she answered.

I left the room and walked down the stairs. Finding the huge wooden doors closed, I pushed them open, then threw myself facedown on the floor.

When I stopped crying, I opened my swollen eyes and found myself staring at a huge mural on the wall. It was a rendering of Jesus teaching the Sermon on the Mount. At the bottom of the picture, in large print, were these words: "Man Tends But God Mends." Those five words came alive inside me. I suddenly knew there was no one on earth I could put my total trust in. Any human being at his or her best will invariably fall short. God alone was my healer.

God is also the great opportunist. He even takes what is

meant for evil and turns it to good. God works through man, but ultimately He does the work that no man could ever do.

All negative emotions about the doctor who made a bad decision disappeared. That momentary medical mistake of misjudgment became an opportunity for a lifelong treasure: trust.

Seeing is not believing; believing is seeing.

Barbara came by later that day, but I didn't tell her what happened. She'd already suffered enough from being caught in the conflict with her father. I was glad to see her and I wanted to comfort her.

When my doctor returned from out of town, he revised the tissue on my right hand. I had to stay longer in the hospital to get that done. During this time Barbara told her parents about our secret relationship. Her dad's response was beyond unfavorable. He threatened to disown Barbara if she didn't break up with me and move to Maryland with them. Barbara's commitment to me was under fire.

When I was able to leave the hospital, I decided to give her and her family a little time to see if things would calm down before I had my talk with her father. I spoke with Barbara on the phone every day, hearing the fiery details of her dad's determination to break her down.

When the showdown came, her father shot multiple questions at me that were difficult to answer.

"What are your goals?" he asked with a razor-sharp edge in his voice. "Do you want to make a million dollars? Five hundred thousand? Tell me."

"Actually, Mr. Newport, my goal is to follow Jesus."

"Well, that's a cop-out if I ever heard one," he said emphatically. "You don't have any real plans, do you?"

Barbara's mother, who had advancing chronic lung disease, came into the room. "What's all this commotion going on?" she asked her husband.

"They're *doing their own thing*," he bellowed, sarcastically quoting a popular hippie phrase of the day.

In the end, Barbara left with me. It was still pretty early in the evening, so we drove off and parked somewhere. She looked at me and laughed. She was not laughing at her parents or her plight. Her laughter sprang from childlike confidence. She trusted me enough to let her parents move without her. That was classic, resolute resolve.

Shortly after I got my bandages off and my stitches out, day came for Barbara's family to load the moving van and head to DC. They fully expected Barbara and her belongings to be in Potomac, Maryland, when they arrived. Her father was confident that she lacked the courage to come out from under his wallet.

But Barbara was not going to do it.

So Barbara was disowned. Her name could not be spoken by anyone in the family, in the house or in any vehicles.

The separation was emotional because of her mother's medical problems and Barbara's tender heart for her mom. Her dad used that as leverage against her heart for me and her commitment to the Lord.

The trial had begun. The prosecutor, the faultfinder, and the accuser of the brethren all had a strong case, and Barbara and I were not in position to defend ourselves. What we needed was the specialist: a Wonderful Counselor.

Twenty-One

Nowhere to Hide

D r. John and I decided to do a little clinic for some of his colleagues who would be attending a plastic surgery seminar. It was still dark outside when Dr. John brought his six experts into my room. The lights were off and I pretended to be asleep as he gave them the medical history of all the work he'd done for me over the past three and a half years.

While they were murmuring about their own ideas of how they would rearrange my body parts, I carefully inserted a plug into the socket next to my bed under my sheet. The room lit up with several black lights. The walls were plastered with psychedelic posters of rock bands and shiny objects that pulsated under the silk fabric that draped the room's walls. All these fancy doctors thought that somebody had given them drugs for breakfast. They were trippin', and my doctor and I were laughing our heads off.

Dr. John introduced me to all of them. I think that morning was the highlight of their fancy seminar.

After Barbara's family moved to DC, she had nothing but her personal clothes. She stayed at a friend's home until I got released from the hospital. I knew of a man who owned some rental properties on the west side of Cleveland. He offered to let us use a house for free to keep vandals from breaking in and doing damage. It was a far cry from her home in Brecksville; it was more like urban un-renewal. People gave us extra dishes and marginal furniture. We had lots of candles for atmosphere, and we did have each other.

Every day we strolled hand-in-hand to the Westside farmers' market to buy our daily ration of fresh vegetables, cheese, and bread. Evenings we would read *Mother Earth News*, a back-to-the-earth wannabe trade magazine. If you believed all the articles, you could grow food anywhere out of anything, make a livable house out of materials that people threw away daily, and create your own electricity. I liked the idea of building and living in a geodesic dome. Now, I'd never been very good at building the Erector set I got for Christmas. But the pictures of other people doing it looked great.

At the end of the summer I received the settlement from my accident. It wasn't a huge amount, but it was a fortune to us. The ideas I had in Jamaica of leaving the rat race became more than a dream for the future.

We went to the Army/Navy store and bought some adventurous jungle-like gear for an extended trip to that Caribbean island. We rented the same cement-block home in the village we had visited six months prior. I talked to a bar owner who offered to let me lease part of his business property, where I wanted to put up a fresh-fruits juice stand facing the beach and an outdoor movie screen in the back.

I no longer wanted to try to change the world. It was bent on spinning out of control no matter what I did. I just want to be the nicest guy in the world and mind my own business.

I contacted a real estate agent who told us about a 107-acre plot of land that was for sale about ten miles from our base camp. Barbara and I and a few of our new acquaintances drove with this man to visit the property. As we walked around the lush acreage studded with banana and mango trees, I drew a mental blueprint for our little kingdom by the sea—a twentieth-century garden of Eden. This place was absolutely perfect.

As the real estate agent led us down a steep mountain path overlooking the ocean, my mind exploded with possibilities. The rest of the group walked a little ahead as I stopped and envisioned a possible site for my geodesic dome. The beauty enraptured me so much that I said out loud, "So this is paradise!"

The minute those words left my mouth, I stopped dead in my tracks. This was the place I had seen in my heavenly vision. It was the same path, the sunlight, the unique flowers. Even my words were exactly the same! My heart beat wildly and I heard the voice within say, *There is no paradise on earth. There is no utopia, and there is no going back to the garden.* The same words I'd heard in my heavenly vision. I had been shown this exact event five years before in my third-heaven encounter.

I had already wired all of our money into a Jamaican bank and was ready to sign papers. But the voice and the revelation of the heavenly encounter called it off.

Barbara was with her friends, laughing about something, but when she saw my face, her expression changed. "What's wrong?"

"I'm not sure. I'll talk to you about it later." I couldn't talk in front of the Jamaican realtor. In the natural, everything seemed to just fall into place. But in the spiritual, something was wrong. God had declared this garden of Eden off limits, and the banana trees and coconut palms were now forbidden fruit.

That night, with laughter bubbling outside and the scent of marijuana everywhere, I told Barbara, "I don't think this is what God wants me to do." Although I didn't go into detail, she could see how shaken I was. Everybody would think I was a total flake for letting go of that land. But that didn't matter. I had to listen to what I heard.

Nearing the end of our three-week stay, a hurricane was projected to pass by two hundred miles to the north of the island, whipping up huge waves and cutting off the power. These normally laid-back people were terrified at the possibility of a hurricane. They had no protection, zero safety forces, and nowhere to hide.

The hurricane lasted three days, which seemed like a fitting end to a canceled dream. My tropical Walden Pond was not to be. Yet I was not disappointed, just mysteriously relieved.

Today that property and those concepts would be worth multiple millions of US dollars. But I've never thought twice because of the impact of the vision and the voice.

We returned to the Columbus, Ohio, airport with only tropical clothes, and the temperature had plummeted.

After we got to Cleveland, Barbara wanted an Irish setter puppy. We found a beauty and named him Abraham. I started poring over real estate ads, looking for country properties. We found an old Victorian farmhouse with a magnificent barn. "Chew Mail Pouch Tobacco" was emblazoned on one whole side of the barn. The property included the house and the buildings with a little over eight acres. We signed on the dotted line, paying cash for it.

Neither Barbara nor I had grown so much as a radish in a Dixie cup. But we had been reading *Mother Earth News*. We figured it'd be easy; just follow the directions.

We moved in to "McBarb Acres" on December 1, 1973. Shortly after, I realized there was something more important than organic vegetables: getting real heat in our drafty old house.

I found a heavy-duty Dodge pickup that had as many scars as I did. Next I got some equipment: shovels, a pickax, a double-bladed ax, tools, rope…basically everything the farm store carried. Barbara and I bought matching overalls, flannel shirts, and fur hats from the Army/Navy store that would keep the heartiest Siberian warm!

Barbara and I talked about the situation with her family living in the DC area. This had been a difficult time for her emotionally, and a lot of negative pressure was coming at me. We felt it was our responsibility to try to bridge the gap. So we decided to take the risk and pay them a surprise visit, hoping to make peace. We took our dog, Abraham.

We knocked on their door in our matching overalls. Her mom opened the door. She was clearly glad to see her daughter. And her father tolerated me. They still had an agenda, but at least we were on talking terms.

Back home, we continued to rummage through dusty antique stores for old stuff to match an old house. I was determined to make our first Christmas together a memorable one. One afternoon while Barbara was taking a nap, Abraham and I snuck out of the house and headed for a tree nursery in Ashland, Ohio. I'd never purchased a Christmas tree before.

Our ceilings were about eleven feet high, so I picked out the tallest and most expensive tree I could find. We put it in the bay window in our parlor. Then we threw ourselves a little housewarming party. Barbara threaded cranberries and popcorn for decorations, and we went through many boxes of silver tinsel and a few new ornaments to decorate this mammoth tree. We bought ourselves all kinds of practical housewarming presents. Barbara, Abraham, and I celebrated the joy of giving and receiving our first Christmas.

March is a wet, cold, muddy month in the heartland of Ohio. Our neighbors down the street were selling their house and moving to Florida. They invited Barbara and me over for dinner and made a deal for us to buy six acres of their land that was adjacent to ours, giving us a total of fourteen acres, all fenced. He also told me he'd make me a great deal on farm equipment: a nice little tractor with all the gadgets and an old manure spreader—my favorite. Barbara had been talking to me for quite a while about one of her lifelong dreams to own her own horse. That dream was now within our grasp. So we bought our first real farm animal: a little red quarter horse we named Shannon.

One day, while I was zooming around on my tractor, Barbara rode her horse up behind me and said, "Mickey, she's lonely."

"Who are you talking about?"

"Shannon. She needs a friend." She was only one and a half years old and had grown up on the family farm where we bought her. So I went back there to see if there was another horse for sale. I'd had a dream as a kid of getting a big black stallion that I would call Cherokee, because I was somewhat sympathetic with the Native Americans.

When I asked the farm owner about his other horses, he pointed to a buckskin Appaloosa standing in the high grass. "That mare is three years old. Never been trained."

"She looks healthy. What's her name?"

"Cherokee," he said. That nailed it for me. She came to our farm.

There was still a nonviolence vibration in me, so I wanted to train her gently. No bit, just a standard halter and two lead ropes. Most of the time I didn't use a saddle. In the evening, I let her go wherever she wanted.

I didn't know what I was doing, but it seemed to be working. Soon my amazing horse could turn figure eights in a small area. If I let her out, in a couple strides we were cantering at full speed. I didn't know it, but Cherokee would become my therapist, my prayer partner, and my faithful friend.

I developed a real prayer life on top of that beautiful horse. I'd always loved the magnificence of the sky. Cherokee introduced me to the beauty of the earth.

I hooked up the tractor to the manure spreader and unloaded tons of old manure onto our garden spot. I plowed and cultivated it, making it the most fertile soil in North America. It felt good to get dirty and tired.

I had just put all the equipment away and was standing by our rusty gate, breathing in the scent of lilacs, as Barbara walked toward me, down the narrow path from our back door. I suddenly remembered my heavenly vision: the gate, the smell of lilacs, and the face I saw. That pretty girl was Barbara! And the feeling of pleasant peace was our new life together on this land. The spirit of the Lord had hidden it from me for the right time. A friend of mine once said, "God doesn't hide things from us; He hides things for us."

Barbara nuzzled next to me and I put my arm around her. That moment was golden.

Friends of ours from Cleveland and Columbus came to visit on the weekends. We took turns riding the horse, and in the evening we played cards around the table. We invented a lifestyle that was somewhere between *Green Acres* and *Alice's Restaurant*. Although I had thought God showed me there was no such thing as paradise on earth, I still wanted a little corner where I could enjoy peace and tranquility. We gave up the garden island of Jamaica, but maybe it was okay to plant such a life in Ohio.

We were not involved with any Jesus freaks in our area, but a mature woman in one of the Cleveland suburbs took an interest in us and our spiritual growth. She showed the ways of God by example and by solid foundation. She taught us how to know the Bible and life for God.

Many nights I was awakened by spiritual dreams. The symbolism in these dreams showed me that I was spiritually dry and hungry.

I soon grew weary of the weekend parties at our farm. I was also running out of money. Riding on Cherokee and praying was far more fulfilling.

Barbara and I planted a huge garden with eighty-four tomato plants. Life got crazy when the tomatoes all ripened about the same time. Barbara learned how to can them, freeze them, and make a year's supply of spaghetti sauce, and still we had to give most of the tomatoes away. We were having a lot of fun as first-year farmers.

I was driving the tractor in the field one day when Barbara ran up to me from behind the house. "Mickey! Dr. Thomas from University Hospital called. He wants you to go to Cleveland immediately so he can do a live transplant surgery on you."

This type of surgery had to be completed within twenty-four hours after the donor died. I took a quick shower. Then Barbara and I made the two-hour drive to the hospital.

I was excited but anxious about this operation. I wasn't afraid of surgery. I'd known this was coming for many years, and I mentally prepared for it. But this was a big deal. I knew how reluctant the eye doctors had been to even attempt anything like this.

Fortunately, because I had so much experience in University Hospital, my lab work was already on record. And I knew the drill for pre-op preparation quite well.

Early in the morning the doctors took me in. I would be awake for this procedure, which took extensive time to set up. A huge suspended stereoscope apparatus above the table surrounded my head with sandbags so I couldn't even twitch during the delicate procedure. Dr. Thomas and another prestigious eye specialist worked together. I concentrated on very slow breathing and not moving so much as my little finger.

After the surgery, the doctor covered my eye with a plastic protector and put a bandage around my head. Barbara was waiting for me back in my room. I had the nurse cover the windows so it would be completely dark. I laid still for seven days. Barbara never left my side. I didn't speak very much. I concentrated on being able to see.

At the end of seven days Dr. Thomas came in and removed the bandage and took off the patch.

"I can see! I can see! It's amazing!"

"What are you saying, Mickey?" the doctor asked. "You see a little light?"

"No, I can see clearly with both eyes." I had been blind in my right eye for five and a half years, and now I could see. Another colossal miracle. The only problem was, I was seeing two of everything, because the muscles in my eye had been flaccid that entire time.

When Dr. Thomas took me back to his eye lab for intensive reexamination, he was astounded. He told me that during the eye operation, when they took off the old cornea, my eye was dead. The pupil was not light reactive and the iris was wrinkled and adhered. Dr. Thomas had whispered to his colleague, "Too bad. Well, at least he'll have some of his old eye color back, even though he won't have any vision."

Dr. Thomas told my plastic surgeon to come up and take a look. He sat in the chair and just shook his head, "There is no way this is supposed to be happening. Dr. Thomas is the best, and he can't explain it."

The delicate operation attached the new cornea by weaving a thread thinner than spider web twenty-three times around the edge. The eye surgeon was so concerned about possible rejection, he left the stitches in for six months for extra insurance.

Barbara and I were so excited, we zoomed back to our little farm, where I got out Cherokee and took off running in celebration. Barbara was mad that I was riding my horse at full speed after having a successful eye operation that wasn't supposed to work. It was crazy and reckless, but I was so close to Cherokee I felt she needed to be part of the celebration.

This was a major installment in my lessons of supernatural healing. I had no idea I was about to go through a process of receiving a powerful lesson of supernatural obedience.

The conflict between the world's influence and the influence of the Spirit of God increased. Practically every time I read the Scriptures, the words jumped off the page, grabbing me by my emotions because they applied so perfectly to me and my circumstances.

But I still often did things with people because it was what *they* liked and what *they* were doing, even though I was growing more determined to live under the guidance of the words of Jesus and the way He lived.

We had a big harvest and did all kinds of canning and freezing. But my interest in farm life was diminishing, and so was our money to support this way of life. I took a part-time job at a public high school, watching the property from 11 p.m. until morning. Every day, regardless of the weather, I went to the barn and rode Cherokee like a warrior. Together we watched the sun come up and I prayed as hard as I could to commit my way to the Lord, but I always seemed to come up short. It may sound corny, but I really think Cherokee could feel my struggle and was helping me make a stand.

I got a phone call from my dear friend Jerry, telling me he wanted Barbara and me to go with him in his private plane to Florida, and then fly commercially to Jamaica to show him and his wife around. As much as I loved to fly and loved Jerry and his wife, I had a strong reluctance to go. But I gave in and went on the trip.

After the four of us arrived in Jamaica, we rented a car and drove the rugged road on the north shore to the village. It was a little busier than when Barbara and I were there last, but still pretty primitive. We went canoeing and snorkeling, ate all kinds of fresh fruit, and drank the world's best coffee. I started to feel less remorseful for taking the trip with Barbara and my friends and tried to enjoy myself.

At the end of the trip I wanted to show my friends a beautiful place a short drive away called Ocho Rios, where people could snorkel down the fresh-water river right into the ocean. When we got to the beach, I went to the bathroom while Barbara, Jerry, and his wife went on ahead to rent snorkeling equipment. In the bathroom, a piece of graffiti hit me dramatically. It said, "There is nothing sweeter than the name of Jesus." There was no other graffiti on that wall, which seemed very unusual.

As I walked out of the bathroom, a man leaning against the wall motioned for me to come toward him. "You didn't go to Vietnam, did you?" he screamed. "You're a coward, and you deserve all of those burns and scars that happened to you!"

Through some kind of evil divination he was mocking and accusing me. I tried to counter his stabbing words by saying something nice, but he spoke other curses to me in the Jamaican language. His words were dark and disturbing.

When I got to the beach, I saw a Rastafarian man standing there. As I walked past him, he shook a stick at me, releasing some kind of incantation. I did not respond.

I looked down and saw a piece of driftwood between my feet. God revealed to me that I was living out another part of the vision I saw in my heavenly revelation.

I spun around 180 degrees and took off at a sprint. As I ran, I vividly recalled what I'd seen six and a half years before. This scene was a literal depiction of spiritually turning from evil and its power by going in the opposite direction.

There was no way I could tell Barbara or my friends what had happened. I was eager to get back home to Ohio.

A short time after that trip, Barbara received a phone call from her mother. She came to me in a panic. "My mom just had a blackout. She needs help."

"Let's pray about it first."

We did. Then we took the last of our money out of the bank to purchase tickets to fly to Washington DC. We didn't tell Barbara's parents that we were coming.

When we arrived, her mother's attitude had changed completely. "What are you doing here?" she snapped. Clearly we were not welcome. Barbara's mother had sworn her to secrecy about the conversation regarding her blackout, making our unannounced appearance difficult to explain. All of a sudden, our noble gesture seemed like a very stupid idea.

Barbara tried to talk to her father discreetly, offering any type of help we could provide for her mom's declining health issues.

"I don't know what you're talking about," he said harshly. "Your mother's fine, and she certainly doesn't need anything from you."

The night before we were scheduled to leave, Barbara and her father had a one-on-one talk. He verbally pummeled her with one thing after another, concluding with, "You're twenty-one and going nowhere. You're a loser and you're living with a loser. Neither of you are ever going to amount to anything."

Her generous heart was rejected, and it got filled with venom.

A short time later Barbara became confused about our relationship and decided to separate from me for a while. A few months before, her father had given her a new economy car for her birthday, so she'd have something to escape in if she needed to. She drove it to her aunt's house, along with most of her personal belongings. I was devastated.

I called her to arrange a visit. She refused. I told Barbara I knew it was God's will and purpose for us to be together. She became even more distant. She left her aunt's house and drove to her parents' suburban home in Washington DC. Barbara's family was glad she was there and gave her carte blanche of everything.

For the first time in many years, I was completely alone. Our house felt empty. Nothing seemed to have any meaning anymore.

I was stripped down naked, and there was nowhere to hide. I had an overwhelming desire to do the will of God, and I was sure that included my life with Barbara.

Days turned into weeks, and it appeared that she wasn't interested in coming back. Some people told me to forget about her and find somebody else. Although well meaning, these people were not on the same page I was on.

Every morning I got up early and drove to a little Catholic church in the country for the six o'clock service. I sat in the last pew and prayed desperately. After a few weeks, I went for three days without eating or drinking anything. I wasn't fasting for spiritual reasons; I was just so full of desperation I couldn't do anything but pray.

One cold day, I put on my ski jacket and went jogging on the horse trails of our property. A memory flashed on the inner screen of my mind. I saw a picture of a friend of mine when we were in grade school. He was on top of another classmate, having punched him several times. The boy on the bottom called out, "I yield." Nobody used words like that, but I knew what they meant.

I got on my knees on that muddy path, looked into the dark skies, and said, "I yield." It was raw and authentic.

As I was walking back to the house, I sat down next to our creek. An evil voice came at me, weaving one web of accusations after another in my mind. With cunning craftiness and twisted boasting, the voice told me I'd caused my own accident, I had mistakenly bought the farm property, all of these events had driven Barbara away, I wasn't real with God, and I was the cause of my own problems. This attack went on for several hours. Paralyzed by the oppressive bullets, I couldn't stop the lies.

Then the voice of the Holy Spirit spoke words from behind me and right through me: "What you did was an act of love." The voice confronted the lies of the enemy and affirmed that buying the property and everything in my life with Barbara was motivated by love. These eight words released a spiritual explosion, blowing that evil entity away from me, our property, and all of my consciousness.

I stood up, wiped the mud off my pants, and marched to the farmhouse. Once inside I got on my knees and told God, "Lord, I know it is Your will that Barbara and I are supposed to be together. But if she won't come back, please protect her and take care of her. And God, I don't know what lies ahead for me, but I'm willing to walk with You wherever You take me. Jesus, I don't want to be a phony. I want to be a follower, right now and forever."

I walked across the street to the truck diner, got something to eat, came back, went to bed, and slept peacefully.

The next morning I called Barbara and noticed a different tone in her voice. The night before I had my encounter with God on the horse trail, a priest had invited her to be a counselor at a retreat center. While I think he had more than a casual interest in her, there she had an encounter with God that changed her life. She went back to her room that night, stood on top of her chair, and under the powerful influence of the Holy Spirit, she wrote an inspired prayer of praise to God and a personal dedication to Him. She was transformed. She asked me to come get her and take her back home—our home.

As I drove to pick her up, I realized that I had to be willing to give up everything, even Barbara. Like Abraham in the Bible, I needed to be willing to sacrifice my "Isaac" to prove to God that I was for real.

While we were apart, God's presence had touched Barbara in a way that was authentic for her. She was so completely outside of my shadow that she came under His.

The Wonderful Counselor blew away the enemy in my life and Barbara's. He showed me that love never fails and love never ends.

Twenty-two

Falling to Heaven

Barbara's parents were dismayed and disappointed when I showed up at their house, but my reunion with her wasn't hindered. In an arduous yet amazing set of divinely orchestrated circumstances, we had separately, but at the same time, said yes to the dealings of God and the power of *His* love to renew *our* love for each other.

These events were a significant milestone for us. This line in the sand had been about six and a half years in the making from the time of the accident, my desperate cry to God, the heavenly revelations, and the powerful healings, miracles, and supernatural encounters I had with the living God.

In the early days of meeting radical people who had come to put their faith in Jesus, the message I received was predominantly about Him being my Savior. I obviously needed to be saved. And I was rescued from every kind destruction, including eternal separation from God. Now I needed to know Jesus as my Lord—the first priority of my life on a daily basis.

When we returned to our farm in Ashland, Ohio, there was a new sense of peace in our relationship, as if some great war had just been settled. Since we had exhausted all of our finances, I found odd jobs to make enough money to pay the bills. When Barbara enrolled in Ashland College, her father was glad that she was at least doing something in his estimation that was "a worthwhile endeavor."

We worked on our garden together, and I still rode the horses, but the constant stream of visitors stopped. Apparently we weren't much fun anymore.

I discovered some Christian television programming on a UHF channel that included an interesting talk show with interviews and personal life stories as well as shows that had intelligent and contemporary teachings that made sense to me.

I started absorbing Scripture. The Bible energized me every time I opened it. It was like working out with spiritual weights. Reading and meditating on the Scriptures made me stronger.

Barbara had a professor who was a strong and patient believer, in addition to being an excellent teacher. She got an A in his class, even though she had never earned high marks as a student before. His personal story of being taken out of the jungles of South America and becoming a college professor was astonishing. We began to meet with him and his wife, and they gave us some wise counsel.

Although he recognized that we were totally committed to each other, he told us it would be honoring and healing to both Barbara's parents and my mother if we got married in the Catholic church.

I realized that Rev. Professor Juan was only interested in helping us on our journey, so I listened to his spiritual wisdom. In this particular case, I had to admit that Barbara's father was right and I'd been wrong. In my idealism, I had resisted a traditional wedding. Eloping had been unorthodox, which had caused difficulty for her family and our future.

Barbara and I felt really good about the idea. And amazingly, her father was not only in hearty agreement, he offered to pay for everything…at the Ashland Country Club!

On that beautiful day, Barbara and I formally committed what we had already done privately.

In the months that followed, as I read the Scriptures and other books that normally would have been complicated to understand due to my lack of training, I discovered a new capacity to learn and understand the things of the Spirit of God. The light of God's illumination was on inside me, and it became more and more energizing.

Coincidentally we began to build relationships with people our age who were radically dedicated to serving the Lord. We were excited to meet people who had bumper stickers saying, "I Found It," "One Way" (with a finger pointing up), and "Jesus Loves You."

When Barbara told me she was pregnant, I was shocked. We had never really talked about having kids, and I'd just started gaining some momentum in taking care of our bills. But she was elated about having a baby.

I got serious about finding a better job, which I did. It provided better money and also some job security.

Barbara had some bleeding in her seventh month, but she was treated and released. Our son, Michael, was born on March 4, 1976, about five weeks premature, five pounds and one ounce, with no apparent problems.

When he was about six weeks old, we attended a sunrise Easter service at a contemporary church called Grace Haven. Phil Keaggy had drawn a map of this place for me, which I had kept on my bookshelf for over five years. We could hardly believe what we found there. Jesus freaks of all ages and races came together with one common interest: they were God crazy and authentically excited to live in community together and to reach other people for Christ. Guitars, flutes, and tambourines combined to make amazing praise music to the Lord. We didn't know there were people who called this going to church! They were about participation, not observation.

Barbara and I really enjoyed all the singing, clapping hands, and dancing as well as praying for one another. When it was over, we didn't want to leave.

One Sunday morning in the fall of 1976, every song and every word I heard in the service was illuminated to me. I knew in my heart that I was supposed to say something publicly, but I had no intentions of doing that. The feeling was so strong that I didn't think it was right for me to take the elements of communion if I didn't respond. I still chickened out.

But before the meeting was dismissed, I stood up and said, "Wait. Stop. I have something to say."

Dead silence.

"I should be dead. I had enough wrong with me to kill ten people. But God saved me and healed me. I shouldn't be sitting in this pew right now. I should be running down the street telling everybody what great things the Lord has done for me!" I dropped down in my seat and put my hands in my face, shaking and weeping.

Suddenly, the whole room went from silence to reverential praise to the one I'd just honored—clumsily, shakily, but powerfully.

I've heard the kingdom of God referred to as an upside-down kingdom. When we are weak, we are made strong. Meekness is not weakness but rather power under control. When you humble yourself, God will propel you forward. I'd just had a firsthand experience in projecting an expression that caused people to explode into praise.

I took it in stride, but as the weeks went by, it happened more and more. The Holy Spirit would inspire me to say things publicly, both in the Sunday morning services and also when we met in small groups in homes, where everybody had a chance to contribute and receive.

One night I was up all night with a high fever, but I wasn't sick. The fever kept me from sleeping for even five minutes, and I was supposed to work twelve hours the next day. Barbara kept telling me, "Honey, I think the Lord wants you to quit that job and trust Him."

The macho man I was knew that I had to be responsible for bringing home the bacon. But Barbara convinced me. The next morning, I called my employer and told them I couldn't come in. Then Barbara put her hand on my forehead and prayed for me. My temperature went away even before she lifted her hand off my sweaty forehead.

I got the message. But how was I going to fulfill my responsibilities and pay the bills? This was especially important now that we had a baby.

The contemporary message of the Jesus Movement contained a strong belief that Jesus was coming back…very soon. For some people, it was so imminent that they felt no need to brush their teeth or floss. But since the bills didn't stop, I couldn't afford to take this attitude.

People began asking me to speak at their churches, business meetings, or other gatherings—to tell my story and to share my understanding from the Scriptures. I never planned on this, nor did I aspire to do this. I was more or less drafted. But when I started speaking, I discovered that this was why I was sent back from heaven. I was given a second chance to fulfill my destiny.

Going to Jamaica was an attempted escape, not only from the reality of my situation but also from God's plan to use me in ways I could never have dreamed. Jesus said, "He who loves his life will lose it, and he who hates his life in this world will keep it for eternal life. If anyone serves Me, let him follow Me; and where I am, there My servant will be also."[18] God was opening doors for me to share my testimony and to teach the Word.

When our son was a few months old, Barbara noticed that Michael's muscles were not developing—he wasn't holding his head up, for example. In every other way, he seemed healthy and happy. He spoke with a large vocabulary for his age, but he was not showing signs of physical support.

We took Michael to the doctor, who diagnosed him with cerebral palsy. It was orthopedic in nature, not intellectual.

We believed God would heal our son. After all, we were walking by faith in every other category of our lives.

I had more and more opportunities to share my testimony in meetings, and I saw the Holy Spirit do many things beyond my ability.

Two years after Michael was born, we had our second child. Matthew was born on Easter Sunday in 1978.

Shortly after that, Michael received additional examinations. The prognosis did not cast a bright outlook for his future. But we continued to trust in God.

After spending some very valuable time at Grace Haven, God directed us to be part of a church in our town of Ashland. They made a leader. Speaking engagements and other invitations continued to increase.

Some of our new friends mentioned they had played progressive/rock music in bands during their teenage years. Together, with me playing guitar, we brought contemporary worship into our church, praising the Rock of Ages with our music.

As we made relationships with other churches throughout the region, our little church grew numerically and spiritually.

While working out at a health club, I overheard a pastor say that he was a counselor at a large reform school in our area. I asked him, "Do you think they would be open to having me share my testimony with the inmates?"

He said they had a new chaplain who was very into trying to

reach these troubled youth. So our band headed to the reform school.

The chaplain said normally about twenty out of the 130 kids there showed up in the gym on Sunday morning. But when they heard the sound check on Saturday night, with guitar, drums, and synthesizers blaring, all 130 showed up the next morning. After we rocked the place, I shared my story. Then we played more music and I invited them to change their lives. Over ninety of those kids came forward to ask Jesus into their hearts.

The gig was supposed to be a one-time deal. But when people heard about what happened, they invited us to play in other places.

We were even asked to perform at the prison where the movie *The Shawshank Redemption* was filmed. This is one of the darkest places you can imagine. The first time we went, a cloud of supernatural love descended on me when those men came in. I felt God's love for each one of them—not some form of brotherly love, but a supernatural love for some pretty unlovely people.

Our little band ended up playing there five or six times a year, and we did a Bible study once a month. It was a mission field right near our home.

A number of years ago, in California, a man approached me. "You won't remember me, but you brought a rock band in when I was in prison. I just want you to know that I've stayed with the Lord all these years from that day." He was now married, had a family and a good job, and he'd received new life. That is miraculous.

Barbara and I had two more children: Jacob in April 1981, and Elizabeth in April 1983. In spite of our faithful prayers, Michael was still not walking. So we reluctantly got him a wheelchair. I cannot describe what it is like as a father to have the firstborn son so severely afflicted. And yet, I don't know anybody who loves life as much as our Michael.

He and his brother Matthew once went on a missions trip to Africa so that Michael could pray for people in the poorest country in the world. I cannot watch the video of their trip without falling apart. Matthew and Michael's gift of charity will not go unrewarded in this world or in the age to come.

Barbara and I will never give up praying for all of our children, but we pray in a special way for Michael. He wants to change the world, and the world needs changing.

In 1977, when Michael was about a year old, I had an astounding dream. I was standing on the porch of our farmhouse, observing a passenger bus that was off the road, stuck deep in mud. The next instant, I was looking through the windows of that bus at the people trapped inside, trying to get out. At the other end of the bus, standing outside, was a famous television minister in a three-piece suit. I was wearing jeans, my boots, and a flannel shirt. I kept watching and waiting for the highly experienced and gifted man to do something spiritual to release these people. But he just stared at me.

I lifted my hand, pointed my finger, and said, "In Jesus' na—" Before I finished saying the word *name,* the windows and doors of the bus popped open, and people were laughing as they were climbing out.

In the dream, I clearly heard the Holy Spirit say to me, "When I start using you to set people free, be careful not to get too excited about it personally or you could go backward." The Bible says it's better to store up treasures in heaven than to take credit for yourself here on earth.[19] I believe we should also expect rewards in this life if we live to please God. Hebrews 11:6 says that without faith it is impossible to please God, "for he who comes to God must believe that He is, and that He is a rewarder of those who seek Him."

Our church in Ashland sent my family to a neighboring small

town called Butler. I was soon given more responsibilities in the new church, as well as numerous opportunities to speak in other churches. Soon we began hosting conferences in various places, helping people to find their special gifts and learn how to use them.

As the kids got older I traveled more. I was even invited to speak internationally, usually in the context of team training. Part of the benefit for me was building relationships with other people involved in ministry who were highly respected but also very real.

Barbara and I both had opportunities to contribute to the lives of people in ways that we knew were significant and long lasting. We sensed there was some kind of change coming, possibly a geographical one, because there was interest in us starting our kind of church in the Cleveland area.

In 1992 Michael had surgery on his back to straighten a spinal curvature that had developed. During this procedure Michael's nerves were damaged. He lost some of his bodily functions, and he was in extreme pain. The doctors claimed there was nothing wrong with Michael and that everything would return, but they didn't. This was an arduous time for us as a family, and it deeply affected Michael. Many people prayed for us. And I researched various places in the nation to try to find therapeutic help for him.

Geographical change did come. We were invited to base our ministry two hours east of Dallas, Texas. The move would be a big step of faith. We'd be laying down our leadership at a great church, giving up our property, and taking the risk of starting anew. But we sensed God was behind this, so we accepted.

Life doesn't always turn out the way we think. God has the ability to reroute us when we need a course correction—like a vehicle's GPS.

We were given space in our new church in Garden Valley, Texas, to set up our ministry. The international ministry really took off.

Barbara and I felt that we should host a conference at our church facility. The leadership really trusted us, but they were a little skeptical that some of our guest speakers may push the envelope to the outer edges.

The conference achieved much more than we could've hoped for. The regular Sunday morning service blended into our three days of celebration and teaching ministry. Toward the end of the worship service, the voice of God surprised me once again. I heard the Spirit say five words to me that were so personally encouraging, I haven't told anybody about them. Those words are a private treasure.

I tried to cover the noise of my crying so I wouldn't disturb all the other people who were caught up in their personal enjoyment of the Lord. When I felt something behind me, I turned and saw Jesus, looking the same as when I saw Him in Canada twenty-four years ago, including the multicolored cloak. But this time his face wasn't sad. He was smiling. He tilted his head slightly and pointed at me. He didn't speak, but the message He communicated was "Way to go, Mick. You're doing what you were sent to do, and you'll keep doing it as long as you follow Me."

Between what the Holy Spirit said and the joy I saw on Jesus' face, is there any higher approval rating a person could have?

I don't dwell on it, but I am aware of the times I've wasted opportunities because of the fear of man rather than being led by the Spirit of God. I believe the mistakes we make are forgiven and forgotten for those who have a yielded heart and are following the Lord. However, it is my opinion that those times that we waste, even though they are erased, could have been filled with some useful endeavor while here on earth. What we do in this life will echo in eternity. That's not a Bible verse, but it is a good concept from the movie *Gladiator* that I think is true.

The majority of the time I've spent serving the Lord has been to the worldwide church, with authentic followers and believers of our Lord. I have a heart for those who are in need, who don't know about the love and power of God. I believe the words of Jesus are true today: "The harvest truly is great, but the laborers are few; therefore pray the Lord of the harvest to send out laborers into His harvest."[20]

One of my favorite talks is called "Being Inconvenienced for God." In it I share examples of when I've had a plan that got interrupted when I encountered another person. Though I've had the privilege of speaking to some fairly large crowds and have even been on television, some of the most dramatic events that I cherish involve God's setups—where He used my life in a strategic way to affect a single life for eternity.

A few years ago I got an e-mail from a person who was prepared to commit suicide. For some reason she clicked on the television just before starting the fatal process. By happenstance she came upon the History Channel, which had a short version of me sharing part of my story. Alarmed, she looked me up on the Internet. Not only did she *not* take her life, she gave it to the Lord.

I've had encounters with people sitting next to me on airplanes whose lives were changed by being healed or receiving some kind of spiritual gift because of God arranging it. Recently I received an e-mail from a man who had been going from church to church, desperately trying to find God. He found my story on the Internet and said he received the Lord and was set free from various types of spiritual oppression.

These kinds of things happen to me many times throughout the year. Obviously I can't take credit for this, with the exception that I've told the Lord I am available.

The prophet Isaiah had an encounter in which he was caught up in heaven and was "undone." He went from human awareness and human weakness to volunteerism. After he was touched by a burning coal from the altar of God, he said, "Here am I! Send me."[21]

Luke 24 records two disciples who met up with Jesus after He had risen from the dead. But they didn't recognize Him. When their eyes were finally opened, they said, "Did not our heart burn within us while He talked with us on the road, and while He opened the Scriptures to us?"[22]

Have you had a heavenly experience, like Isaiah? Or have you been unaware that Jesus is walking alongside you, like those disciples? I pray that this book will inspire you to have a burning heart for the Lord and cause you to be a carrier of His fire as you continue the process of falling to heaven and sharing God's love wherever you go.

Twenty-three

Eternity:
The Final Frontier

"E very man dies. Not every man really lives." This dramatic quote
by Mel Gibson portraying William Wallace in the movie *Braveheart* can have a variety of different interpretations. If I apply it to
my life, I could say it this way, as I did earlier in this book: "Hardly
anyone dies and is given a second chance to really live."

The common denominator that unites all human beings is
that everyone is born and everyone will die. There remain only
two possibilities after death: an afterlife or oblivion—a never-
ending state of nothingness. The most common conclusion
drawn from the latter line of thinking is that there is no God.
Unquestionably I've experienced the reality of an afterlife and,
more important, an ongoing dramatic love relationship with the
true, living God.

Regardless of what a person's beliefs are, everyone will cross
the threshold at death and enter into the adventure I refer to as
"The Final Frontier." I do not want to be too lighthearted about
something as serious as life, death, and the afterlife, but I like
what comedian Woody Allen said: "It's not that I'm afraid to die,
I just don't want to be there when it happens."[23] The truth of the
matter is, whether young or old, conscious or unconscious, everybody will be at this frontier when it happens.

I know for certain I was sent back here to fulfill a purpose—one I desperately bargained for. That purpose is not about death, but rather about the fullness of life. This purpose has taken me all over the world, logging over 2.5 million airline miles as my wife and I have traveled to some of the great cities of the world. At this point in my life there's one thing I am certain of: the honor and value of each individual human life.

There was a time when I thought, *Life is short, so hurry up and get as much out of it as you can.* But now I believe that life is short, so we should live each day with authentic appreciation, knowing we have the opportunity to be lights in a dark world.

I've been asked, "Do you think these are the last days? Is the end of the world at hand?" I can say this with 100 percent assurance: you are closer to the end of the world than you were when you started reading this book!

In recent years, we have been fed a steady diet of bad news. The attack on the Twin Towers on 9/11. Natural disasters such as the Japanese earthquake, followed by a tsunami, followed by a nuclear power disaster. The economic crisis in 2008. The constant division and rhetoric in governments that represent instability instead of solidarity. The injustice of human slavery, including global sex slavery and the profiteering of drug slavery. Child soldiers and other inconceivable human brutality. Graphic violence, such as the horror of school shootings and global terrorism. And we are gradually becoming desensitized into accepting all this as normal. These travesties are anything but normal.

While it's easy to point out the problems, what we need are solutions. Discerning what's wrong is part of turning to what is right. For me, I have found answers by turning to the Source of all wisdom. Throughout all of my personal challenges—and there has been some really serious stuff—I have found the unfailing goodness of God in the midst of chaos and apparent instability.

When all hope and possibilities were gone, I had a supernatural encounter with the Lord of Lords. The things I saw and experienced did not come from my subconscious mind as a result of hysterical imagination unleashed by trauma. To wake up in a dead body by the power of God and for no earthly reason to be at peace and full of love is inconceivable, except for the miraculous power and mercy of the eternal God. To this day I still assert—as loudly as I can—that the greatest experience of all is the personal love and care of the Father, the Son, and the Comforter, the Holy Spirit.

We were all born in a spirit war that cannot be fought using natural abilities. Denying it or ignoring it doesn't make it go away. We need spiritual armor and spiritual training to know how to withstand, protect, and overcome the tactics of our enemy.

Is there such a thing as spiritual warfare? Are there evil personalities in the spirit realm, including Satan? Unequivocally, the answer is yes. Throughout this story, you have read about a great wrestling between the realm of darkness and the Spirit of God. I believe, in my case, there was a dual agenda by these forces of darkness: to lead me away from the purposes for which I was sent back, and to be pervasively destructive in every area of my life, including my mind.

Because I was shown approximately six and a half years of my future in the heavenly vision, does that mean that all lives are predetermined? In my opinion, no. Our lives are continually full of choices. The decisions we make have a direct result on the lives we live and in the lives of others.

It is also my opinion that even though we have a free will, God can sovereignly intervene and block some wrong choices. I know that His "messing around with my plans" prevented me from accidents, wrong relationships, and hidden traps. And there are undoubtedly a multitude of things in the unseen world that never occurred because Jesus is the best Shepherd.

Would I have found faith in God if I had not been in an accident? It's only speculation, but I certainly wasn't headed in that direction. I had a close call, and that is the understatement of my life!

I've also been asked, "Don't you regret all the suffering and all the things you lost?" I've received back much more than I had prior to having the Lord reveal Himself to me. Concerning regrets, I am forgetting what's behind so that I can press on to what's ahead, the upward expectation of greater things in this life to experience and to receive, so that I have real power to give.[24]

The ways of God are unlike our ways. Everything about following Him takes supernatural ability. On the day I slipped through this earthly dimension into God's glory in heaven, I discovered something that would change me forever: the reality of eternal life. Not until I experienced true brokenness did I know how much I needed the Lord. I'd spent my energy looking for ways to get my act together. God isn't looking for people who have their act together; He wants people who know their act is over!

There are at least four differences about how I came to be a follower of the Lord Jesus compared to a lot of other people.

One, I didn't know I was lost. A lot of people hear messages about the need to be "saved" and have a relationship with the Lord before they die so they will go to heaven. When an individual is convinced that he or she is lost, the gift of eternal life is activated and that person receives eternal life. That is probably how the vast majority of people respond to the good news about Jesus and the kingdom of God. That's not how it happened for me. I cried for mercy not to die because I wanted to live. Then I burst into heaven and came back to earth full of God Himself and the River of Life.

Two, for some time I had no one to talk to or guide me in my spiritual understanding relative to my experiences and the

243

Falling into Heaven

insight I was receiving. The good part of this is that I was not being humanly influenced, so it was completely outside my own understanding. I was isolated in a hospital and focusing on life-and-death circumstances and healing. Restoration was a high priority on God's list, as well as for the medical staff and my family. The vast majority of people who become followers of the Lord have been invited by someone and are surrounded by a support group. They receive a foundation of their faith as they grow with others. Participation in some kind of a church group is the usual way in which a person receives life in the Spirit and has opportunities to express it.

Three, I have been strategically positioned in various impulses of the Holy Spirit. I have had the privilege of intimately knowing some of the best teachers, leaders, and incredibly gifted people all over the world. A number of years ago, while we lived in Ohio, I was driving the car by myself and the Holy Spirit told me, "Mickey, I've given you the best." I smiled and felt really good about that for about fifteen minutes. Then I remembered, "To whom much is given, from him much will be required."[25] Then I felt the sober sense of divine responsibility.

Four, most people who are in full-time ministry go through some kind of a conventional routing. They go to Bible school, seminary, or some kind of formal training. That was not my course of action. I've had a lot of training from some of the best contemporaries of mine for over forty years, and I consider myself a seasoned beginner and follower of an amazing mystic: Jesus Christ, the Messiah.

Besides the uniqueness I just mentioned, I consider myself an ordinary person who has experienced extraordinary things from the incredibly generous and personal God of the universe.

People ask me, "What kind of minister are you?" I've worn many hats, but one of the most primary and important role is that I am a messenger. I carry a message of hope to all people for any situation. I've had the privilege of being a source of encouragement to people all over the world—many times up close and personal, and sometimes to people I will never meet. Encouragement can be more than a cheerful building up. I have had the privilege of being an instrument to impart spiritual bravery through the release of power that I can only credit to the Anointed One in me.

My hope is about the power of God in this life and the continuation of life in the afterlife and the age to come. I'm an example of a deathbed encounter that included the grace to save me and register me as a citizen of heaven. Some have talked about foxhole religion, or religion being a crutch. Religion may be a crutch, but I have found the authentic power of God to be a total life-support system, which is still sustaining me today. There are millions of stories about people receiving God's merciful intervention when they are in a crisis and desperately cry out to God.

The question "If you died tonight, do you know that you would go to heaven?" has been used countless times to confront people with the reality of eternity. I don't want to dispute the importance of facing the reality that all humans are mortal. But I would rather align myself with the Lord Jesus when He said that his Father "is not the God of the dead, but the God of the living."[26] Some believe eternal life begins with human death. Jesus said, "And this is eternal life, that they may know You, the only true God, and Jesus Christ whom You have sent."[27]

Eternal life begins in this life, while you are alive. My experiences are personal and subjective. Yet I am persuaded that if I had died in the ambulance en route to the first hospital, I would've gone to heaven to be with the Lord. Why can I say that? Because it is written, "Whoever calls on the name of the Lord shall be saved."[28] My prayer, "God, I'm sorry, please give me another chance," released His mercy, which cleansed me and would have taken me into His presence had I died in the emergency room or on the operating table. The moment the words came from my lips, I inherited new-creation life, everlasting life, not just a resuscitated biological life.

I am also persuaded that it is through Jesus that any person is transferred from darkness into the kingdom of the Son of the Father's love. I am convinced that no one, including me, can judge who will or will not be accepted into heaven. God alone is the Judge of who shall receive everlasting life. It is, however, incumbent upon us to know the difference between right and wrong, good and evil.

As I have thought about the dynamics of death and dying while preparing this book, I realized anew that some of what I have seen is very intense. I thought, *I want to be mindful that I don't scare somebody.* Then I thought, *Hey, some of this stuff scares me!* If anybody could scare someone concerning their need to make sure they go to heaven, it would be me. I've got the information and the ammunition. But I would rather "love the hell out of you" by sharing the message of hope in Jesus and let the Holy Spirit do His work. What I mean is that I prefer to address the bad stuff that leads people astray through love and compassion instead of through fear.

I live in the Bible belt of America. Many people here were raised in an inherited belief system. In some cases, their faith tradition has been in the family for generations. I'm sure I am not the only one who was raised in church but never had a real encounter with the power of God.

No matter how many thousands of messages I've preached, conferences I've taught, or positions I've held, I am most known for my failed death. I didn't know it then, but what happened to me is called an NDE—a near-death experience. I believe many people have had an NLE—a near-life experience. They've been in church, have done the expected things, adhered to certain traditional behaviors, yet have never had the transforming experience that is called being born from above.[29]

A wealthy young man once ran up to Jesus in public and asked Him, "What shall I do that I may inherit eternal life?"[30]

Jesus answered, "You know the commandments," then listed six of the ten commandments.

The man replied, "All these things I have kept from my youth."

Feeling a great love for him, Jesus said, "One thing you lack: Go your way, sell whatever you have and give to the poor, and you will have treasure in heaven; and come, take up the cross, and follow Me." The Bible says that he went away sad because he had great possessions.

This man had a near-life experience. The Lord told him he could have treasure in heaven, but he wouldn't untangle himself to be free to follow Jesus. There's a big difference between going to church and being an all-in follower of Jesus Christ, actively led by the Spirit.

Why did Jesus say, "I am the way, the truth, and the life. No one comes to the Father except through Me"?[31] I spent years examining all kinds of belief systems and have had the privilege of traveling all over the world. And all I know is this: I was blind and now I see. I was crippled, and now I can walk. I did not have leprosy, but I had really bad skin problems that got healed. I was pretty dead, and now I am alive. My heart was broken and I never thought I'd never be able to love again. My heart is now healed and the love of God floods my heart. I had no hope; now I have hope every day, in this world and into the next. If there were a forensic study on how these things happened in my life, the fingerprints would belong to Jesus Christ.

Jesus' Father sent Him on a mission to seek and save those who were lost. On that mission He was to destroy the works of the enemy. He single-handedly liberated billions from captivity. And he is still ruling from the highest seat of government in heaven. For over four decades the Lord has been popping up in my life, doing miraculous things. I keep hearing about astounding proofs for God's existence in this country and every corner of this beautiful yet desperate planet. There is a preponderance of evidence that the source of everything is Jesus, who is the same yesterday, today, and forever.[32]

Jesus earnestly wants people to know Him. He performed miracles as evidence that He was who He claimed to be. The mercy I received and the signs and wonders that changed my life have come from the Lord, not from any natural source. I received power to be a living witness, and I want everyone to receive the greatest treasure anyone can ever obtain.

The title of this book, *Falling into Heaven,* is a dual reference to the temporary pleasure of being in free fall as a skydiver and to positioning oneself to access the gate into heaven. Unlike every other belief system, the answer is not becoming a spiritual master. It is in humbling ourselves before the Master of all spirits. Jesus said, "I am the door. If anyone enters by Me, he will be saved."[33]

Jesus also said, "Blessed are the poor in spirit, for theirs is the kingdom of heaven."[34] Humility does not indicate a mind-set of how crummy, impoverished, or worthless we are; rather that we are passionate seekers of Him who has the bread to satisfy our spiritual hunger. Humility is not a solitary prayer to get forgiven so that we are made right with God. It is part of a lifestyle we live in private with the Lord and among the people we encounter. The Bible is clear that if we humble ourselves before the Lord, He will lift us up.[35]

Prayer is an acknowledgment that we need more than what

we have. People who place their trust in natural things—who are strong and self-sufficient in their own power—don't think they need prayer.

The most important person talking during prayer isn't you. Followers of Jesus need to hear His voice and, more important, obey Him. I have discovered a condition: chronic obedience, which should be a part of every maturing believer's life. I'm sure that every person who chooses to frequently, habitually, and joyfully obey the Lord will have the most adventurous life there is.

It is vital to be filled with the wisdom of the Scriptures. It is essential to be around people whose heart is on fire with passion for Jesus. It is rewarding to see the power of God's love touch someone else's life. There are thousands of people within your reach who need a miracle, a word of encouragement, healing, a good laugh, or just a real friend.

My identity is not as a skydiver and a stock trader, or even a Christian and a minister. I have operated in the gifts of God, seeing some amazing things. I have endured suffering physically, emotionally, and spiritually with great perseverance. But my true identity is that I am a son of the living God and I am in relationship with Him.

I passionately invite you to experience God and to know His love and power. You may fall into one or more of the following categories today:

- You are outside the kingdom and you need Jesus, the Gate, to receive you and bring you in.

- You have been in a church of some kind or part of a belief system. Perhaps you've never had a powerful encounter with the God of Abraham, Isaac, and Jacob. All of the Old Testament prophets pointed to the epicenter, Jesus the Messiah in the glory of His death and resurrection.

- You have at one time known the Lord, but you've drifted away and need to be reawakened.

- You were once a follower of the Lord, but have fallen away because of sin and need to turn from that and return to Him.

- You need a miracle, a healing, or relational reconciliation.

- You need spiritual renewal and to be energized by God the Holy Spirit.

- You need to be set free from fears, emotional problems, bad habits, or a broken heart.

Regardless of your condition, I have a message for you: the kingdom of heaven is at hand now. You can access God by opening your heart and praying a prayer of faith with your own words. Your prayer can be about any of what I mentioned above, or other things important to you.

Below is a prayer that I invite you to pray with me out loud. Make these words your own, then keep praying. Whatever words come out will be living words. The Holy Spirit helps us to pray according to the will of God.

Jesus, thank you that you came to seek and save the lost. I'm lost, I need to be saved, and I ask for your mercy. Give me another chance. Forgive me in every way that I have fallen short of your unique and special design for my life. Fill me with your spirit of wisdom and revelation to authentically know you personally and powerfully. Lord Jesus, I want the same power that has changed Mickey's life to change mine. I open my heart to you. Come and be both Lord and Savior of my life. Holy Spirit, I ask that you would activate your gifts and the fruit of your Spirit in my life in an accelerated way, so that I experience more of your power working in me as I yield to you. I do yield to your will for my life and I ask that you would grant me the courage to set myself apart to be a useful instrument for You, to touch lives all around me wherever you send me for the rest of my life. Holy Spirit, Jesus said you would be my Guide. Guide me supernaturally in all your ways. Thank you for the eternal life you give to me—in this world and the next. You say that I will never perish, and no one will ever snatch me out of your loving hand. [Continue with your own prayer.]

On June 10, 1963, John F. Kennedy made a commencement speech at the American University, just months after our country nearly went to nuclear war with Russia. He was contending for peace in the world. He said:

In the final analysis, our most basic common link is that we all inhabit this small planet. We all breathe the same air. We all cherish our children's futures. And we are all mortal.[36]

These words are true, but they are not confining. Although we are all mortal, we can put on immortality and pass into that final frontier by falling into heaven and finding our address in the celestial city.

About the Author

A plane crash in 1968 consumed half of Mickey's body in third-degree burns. Mickey entered heaven and was given a mission to bring a life-giving message of hope back to Earth. Since his second chance at life, Mickey has been a public speaker nationally and internationally. In addition to his personal appearances, his dramatic life story and additional messages of hope have been broadcast on TV and radio. In August 2010 a portion of Mickey's testimony was part of a two-hour special on the highly acclaimed History Channel. It has been broadcast multiple times in the U.S. and other nations with overdubs in their own languages. For over three decades, his message of encouragement and hope has continued to change lives and inspire people of all ages.

You may contact Mickey using the information below.

Mickey Robinson
P.O. Box 682485, Franklin, TN 37068-2485
www.mickeyrobinson.com

Facebook:
www.facebook.com/mickeyrobinsonauthorspeaker

Twitter:
@Mickey_Robinson

Acknowledgements

I would first like to recognize the multitudes of people who I may never see but heard my story and responded very kindly to me and to the story. I've learned that each individual life has immense value. Thank you for making my story a part of yours. I would also like to thank all the nonconformists—people who have discovered their own uniqueness and express it in such diverse and colorful ways. The apostle Paul wrote, "And do not be conformed to this world, but be transformed by the renewing of your mind."[37] You have been a constant reminder to me to be true to myself in the ongoing journey.

To Francis Frangipane who first encouraged and enabled me to write the story so many years ago and for being a good example of practicing what you preach. Chloe Lovejoy, more than writer, you are a master storyteller and a trusted friend. The times we shared crafting the original version was a lot of fun and is a cherished treasure. James Goll, thank you for so many things practical, but even more for your friendship. To Carlton Garborg and Jerry Bloom for believing in this project and hopefully many more. Special recognition to David Sluka for his long hours of work with much patience and encouragement. Thank you.

For all the people in so many places who supported us generously and at times quite miraculously. To Dennis and Susan Freeman, love is commitment; the deepest thanks for yours. Rick and Eileen Jones for faith, patience, wisdom, and warm fellowship. Dan and Ann Foster, you gave us a break in the middle of this writing and also reminded us that what we experienced in the past still exists now.

There are so many more people and places. We will carry all of you in our hearts. We need your love, prayers, and encouragement.

In the final analysis, all thanks belong to the Lord Jesus the Messiah. You have done all these wondrous things and will help us all to finish well. I am truly grateful.

Endnotes

1 These are the first and last lines by aviator and poet John Gillespie Magee, Jr., from his sonnet *High Flight*, written a few months before his death during a mid-air collision in World War II.

2 Proverbs 27:20.

3 Psalm 16:11.

4 Revelation 22:1.

5 Luke 23:4.

6 Genesis 1:1.

7 Ephesians 3:10.

8 2 Corinthians 12:2.

9 Philippians 4:7.

10 Luke 17:21.

11 Genesis 1:1–5 KJV.

12 Matthew 5:7.

13 Proverbs 17:22.

14 Numbers 11:23.

15 Isaiah 60:17.

16 John 10:10.

17 Isaiah 64:6 NASB.

18 John 12:25–26.

19 Matthew 6:19–21.

20 Luke 10:2.

21 Isaiah 6:1–8.

22 Luke 24:32.

23 Woody Allen, *Without Feathers,* "Death (A Play)" (New York: Random House, 1975), 99.

24 Philippians 3:7–14.

25 Luke 12:48.

26 Mark 12:27.

27 John 17:3.

28 Romans 10:13.

29 John 3:3.

30 Mark 10:17–25.

31 John 14:6.

32 Hebrews 13:8.

33 John 10:9.

34 Matthew 5:3.

35 James 4:10.

36 http://www.pbs.org/wgbh /americanexperience /features/primary-resources /jfk-university/.

37 Romans 12:2.